THE
WOBBIT

A PARODY

THE HARVARD LAMPOON

A TOUCHSTONE BOOK

Published by Simon & Schuster

New York   London   Toronto   Sydney   New Delhi

Touchstone
A Division of Simon & Schuster, Inc.
1230 Avenue of the Americas
New York, NY 10020

First Touchstone trade paperback edition November 2013

TOUCHSTONE and colophon are registered trademarks of Simon & Schuster, Inc.

For information about special discounts for bulk purchases, please contact Simon & Schuster Special Sales at 1-866-506-1949 or business@simonandschuster.com.

Cover illustration by Andrew Farley
Map of Widdle Wearth by Jonathan Finn-Gamiño

The Simon & Schuster Speakers Bureau can bring authors to your live event. For more information or to book an event contact the Simon & Schuster Speakers Bureau at 1-866-248-3049 or visit our website at www.simonspeakers.com.

Manufactured in the United States of America

10   9   8   7   6   5   4   3   2   1

ISBN 978-1-4767-6367-5
ISBN 978-1-4767-6392-7 (ebook)

Dedicated to John Marquand,
our wobbit

CONTENTS

PREFACE

For everyone who has delighted in J. R. R. Tolkien's fantasy masterwork—or anyone who's just looking for a good laugh—this is the million-copy-selling comic extravaganza that will convince lovers (and haters) of fantasy that they've finally experienced it all and that they'll never need to read another fantasy parody again.

Anyways, that's the slug line we used for *Bored of the Rings*, the fantasy parody we published in 1969 that ended the fantasy parody genre. So here's another. Please buy a million copies of this one too, because after this we're out of ideas.

Sincerely,
The Harvard Lampoon

And What Is a Wobbit?

Wobbits are little people, smaller than Little People. They love peace and quiet and food, especially food—meats, poultry, fish, carbs, dairy, and, of course, meats. Berries too. Botanically speaking, a berry is any simple, fleshy fruit produced from a single ovary. It may surprise you to learn that many fruits we don't commonly think of as berries—bananas, avocados, tomatoes, and even pumpkins and watermelons—are actually true berries. Oranges, kumquats, lemons, and other juicy fruits one might peel fall under the category of modified berries. Even more surprising, though, is that some of our most cherished, every-day berries are not berries at all. Blackberries and raspberries are properly classified as aggregate fruits (they contain seeds from different ovaries of a single flower), while mulberries are multiple fruits (easy enough to remember) because they incorporate multiple flowers packed closely together. Even the beloved strawberry is not an actual berry—it is an accessory fruit, so called because the part you eat is not generated by the

AND WHAT IS A WOBBIT?

ovary. Meanwhile, in the category of just-because-they're-funny names, apples and pears are called pomes, and olives, plums, peaches, cherries, and anything else with a pit around the seed are called drupes.

Great. And What Is a Wobbit?

I don't know, why don't you read the stupid book you just bought? Idiot.

A Note to Readers

In this version several minor inaccuracies, most of them noted by readers (without whom, we acknowledge that books could not happen), have been corrected. For example, the text on pages 38 and 39 now corresponds exactly with the runes on the map in the front of this book that were written in a font that was supposed to be impossible to read. Thank you, trollhunter44 of lotr.wikia.com, for pointing this out. More important is the matter of chapter five, which was originally lifted directly from my dream journal and was not intended to be the foundation of 1,200 more pages of literature. There the true story of the Riddle Game is given, as it was eventually revealed (under pressure, which is now retroactively relevant) by Billy to Dumbledalf, according to the *Purple Book*, an entire book I had to write to correct this problem. This is in place of the version Billy first gave to his friends and actually set down in his diary (which, even though I never mentioned it, I can assure you exists, trollhunter44). This departure from truth on the part of a most honest wobbit

was a portent of great significance. That's right, trollhunter44,
your tireless work has resulted in a portent of great significance. I'm sure that makes it all worthwhile. It does not,
however, concern the present story, and those who in this edition make their first acquaintance with wobbit-lore need not
trouble about it. Please, save the troubling for trollhunter44,
who will save us all. An explanation of this apparent inconsis-
tency lies in the history of the anklet, as it was set out in the
chronicles of the *Purple Book* or *The Similarillian,* or wherever
the hell I put it, and is now told in *Bored of the Rings*. Thank
you, trollhunter44, for your loyal patronage, and I hope the
Moblin whose dialogue you made me alter on page 51 kills
you in your sleep.

THE
WOBBIT

I

An Unexpected Trilogy

In a hole in the ground there was stuck a wobbit. Not a stupid, useless, wet hole that you might dig at the beach because your parents drove all the way out here and your dad said that sandcastle set cost twenty damn dollars so you're just going to have to make holes and you'll like it, dammit, nor yet a desperate, useful, dry hole you might dig twenty-eight years later at that same beach because you were just trying to get your dad to respect your career choices and you can't have this on your record just as they were about to move you off of beef-coloring duty at the local Taco Knell. No, this was a wobbit-hole, and that, dear reader, means various things depending on your Google Image SafeSearch preferences.[*]

The hole had a perfectly round door like a doughnut, glazed like a doughnut, with a smaller, half-eaten jelly doughnut

---

[*] When googling words in this book, the publishers recommend the SafeSearch preference "Stupidly Innocent." The *Harvard Lampoon* is made up of upstanding, virginal college students who have worked hard to maintain both their upstandingness and their virginity.

stuck in the exact middle. This was meant to replace the door-knob the wobbit had eaten in an unfortunate (but all too common) jelly-donut-doorknob-switcheroo. The door opened onto a tube-shaped hall, which was like an underground bowl-ing lane, inclined and polished at just the right angle so that, having expended all his limited energy opening and/or eating his way through the door, the wobbit could simply roll himself down the hall in a prediabetic stupor and burp-bounce his way into any of the many round doors opening out of it. No going upstairs for the wobbit: bedrooms, bathrooms, pantries, sit-ting rooms, kitchens, dining rooms, pausing rooms, breakfast nooks, mouthbreathing facilities, lunch-meat storage areas, sweating chambers, cheese lockers, and mirrorless Tempur-Pedic gorging zones—all were on the same floor. "Floors" was, in fact, an utterly meaningless term in Wobbottabad, ever since the city council outlawed stairs for implying an impracti-cal amount of effort and escalators for basically being passive-aggressive stairs.

Now, this wobbit was a very stuck wobbit, and his name was Billy Bagboy. The Bagboys had lived in the neighborhood of Wobbottabad for far longer than anyone could remember, while steadfastly retaining the shortest life spans of any of their neighbors. People considered the Bagboys very respect-able, not only because they had a rather delightful job where they could take secret bites of everybody's groceries, but also because they were almost completely immobile and, even better, unsurprising. You could tell what a Bagboy would say on any question without the bother of taking the mayo-cake out of his mouth, as the answer was almost invariably, "Yum. Mayo-cake."

The mother of our particular wobbit—what is a wobbit?

I suppose wobbits need some description at this point, as the very act of you reading this book in printed form shows that you must be nowhere near a viable Wi-Fi network. According to Legend, a particularly chatty man sitting across from me in Starbucks who has a hat that says "BACKWARD" on the front and ironic tattoos of gauges on his earlobes, the wobbits used to be much like us. Then came the wobesity epidemic, so named because wobbits wobble but don't fall down (until they do, then they usually give up and that's pretty much the end of that). Their cankles became canktellas, and their canktellas became canktellocks. Their muffin tops met their sausage bottoms, and they became scornful and judgmental of the Vertical People, or total flatties, as they call us. Wobbits have no beards, but they have hair everywhere else on their bodies because Gillette's combination razor-blade/backscratcher can only reach so far. They wear no shoes since their Crocs melded with their feet. There is little or no magic about wobbits, except the ordinary gastrointestinal sort, which helps them to digest the bones of the various fish, birds, and marsupials that periodically hopped in from the wild seeking a zoo. Basically, what I'm trying to say is that these guys are really, really fat.

As I was explaining, the mother of this wobbit—of Billy Bagboy, that is—was the famous Instadonna Gram, one of the three remarkable daughters of the old Tele Gram, head of the wobbits who lived across the Street, a distance which seemed just significant enough to call a different town and be done with it. It was often said that long ago one of the Gram ancestors must have taken a Pilates class. Such a tale was, of course, absurd, but certainly there remained something not entirely wobbitlike about them, and once in a while members of the

Gram clan would go and have YOLOs.* They discreetly disappeared, and the family ignored their hashtags; but the fact remained that the Grams were not as respectable as the Bagboys, though they undoubtedly got more likes.

So it happened that one fateful morning (which is really more like fateful 1:30 p.m. in Wobbottabad), Billy Bagboy was stuck in the doughnut-door of his wobbit-hole. This happened just about exactly as often as one might expect, so every sensible wobbit kept a pipe to smoke and a preheated wobburrito to munch on under his doormat as he waited for the cracking wood grain to finally give way. Billy was a respectable wobbit, of course, so the pipe was entirely medicinal wobbit weed, prescribed to combat the chronic no-hungries that afflicted so many wobbits from time to time. It was just then—as Billy was considering whether or not it was possible to take a bean and cheese and wobbit weed hit through his wobburrito—that Dumbledalf came by.

Dumbledalf! If you had heard only a quarter of what I have heard about him, and I have only made it through, like, half of the fourth book, you would be prepared for any sort of remarkable tale—literally any sort, as Dumbledalf was getting up there in years, and he tended to get a bit confused at times. However, all the unsuspecting Billy saw that morning was an old man with a staff. He was tall, thin, and very old, judging by the silver of his hair and beard, which were long enough to tuck into his belt. He was wearing a tall pointed blue hat, long robes, a long grey cloak, a purple cloak that swept the ground, a silver scarf over which his long white beard hung down below his waist, and immense, high-heeled, buckled black

---

* I suppose YOLOs need explanation as well, but whatever. You'll figure it out.

boots. It was all simultaneously unoriginal and a bit confusing, but one thing was absolutely clear: this guy was pretty gay.

"Hey, man," said Billy, and he meant it. Dumbledalf was a man, and "hey" was the least you could say to a person before they left you alone with your food. But Dumbledalf just looked at him from under his long bushy eyebrows and through his half-moon spectacles and over the cat he had found on the street, from whom he was currently trying to obtain spoilers for season four of *Downton Abbey*.

"What do you mean?" Dumbledalf said. "Do you wish to greet me, or mean to identify me as a man made of hay; or are you making a short list of things you might see in a typical barnyard; or simply writing the chorus of a hit folk-rock single?"

Billy had never in his life been accused of doing much of anything, much less four things, all of which sounded like a bit much. It didn't help that he had inhaled a good quantity of hardened cheese, which he now proceeded to choke on. Meanwhile, grumbling that he could never find the damn power button on these Transformers, Dumbledalf tossed the cat into the air. As the laws of probability and surface area would dictate, the cat landed on Billy's stomach, dislodging the hunk of cheese onto the grass before him.

"Very pretty!" said Dumbledalf. "But I have no time to trade cheese this morning. I am looking for someone to share in a YOLO that I am arranging, and it's very difficult to find anyone. Even my Grindr spell came up empty!"*

---

* Dumbledalf's Grindr spell usually allowed him to locate any new or slightly used blenders in the area, which he would then use to make fruit smoothies. He would be no less lonely then, but at least he would have a delicious fruit smoothie.

"I should think so—in these parts! We are plain, fat folk. We don't want a photo and we certainly don't want any YOLOs. Nasty, unpleasant things. Somewhere between a Carpe Diem and a DGAF, with half the intelligence of the former and twice the effort of the latter. I can't see what anyone sees in them," said our Mr. Bagboy, and with a giant bite of his wobburrito, he managed to snap himself out of the doorframe. He went about trying to put his door back up, pretending to take no more notice of the old man, which would have been easier if Dumbledalf had not taken an extreme interest in licking the back of Billy's head.

"Just as I suspected: you're a wizard, Hairy!"

"I am not! My name is Billy Bagboy, and I am a wobbit!"

"Is that so?" Looking puzzled, Dumbledalf spat out Billy's hair and began to chew on his own beard. A look of delight broke out on his face. "Just as I suspected: I'm a wizard, Hairy! I wonder what type of wand I'll get."

Billy had had quite enough of this by now. "Sorry! I don't want any YOLOs, or hair tasting, and I just remembered I left the oven on and the microwave on and the stove off, which is a problem because now I won't have any pancakes to go with my pot roast and popcorn. So good-bye, and you and twelve of your closest friends should all come gorge yourselves in my home sometime soon." Billy didn't mean this last part of course, but it was only polite in wobbit society to propose a gorging whenever one ends a conversation. With that, he pulled the door shut, passed out, and rolled down the hallway in a trail of his own sweat.

Dumbledalf, in the meantime, was still standing outside the door, and laughing long but quietly. Then he ran full speed at the door, leaving a symbolic lightning-bolt crack in the door and a nonsymbolic, amorphous bloody smear on his forehead. He picked himself up and, muttering something about improper fractions, limped slowly away in search of somewhere else to be a wizard.

The next day Billy had almost forgotten about Dumbledalf, as short-term memory loss is a common complication of type 2 diabetes. He spent the whole day building a bird feeder that would feed him birds at the exact rate of his ability to swallow those birds, and he had almost gotten the calibrations right when there was a tremendous knock on the door. Remembering Dumbledalf, he quickly ate three more crows and ran to the entrance, stopping only three times along the way to catch his breath.

"I'm sorry to keep you waiting!" he was going to say, but instead he blurted out, "Black person! Black person!" and quickly closed and locked the door. Of course, this was the same door that Billy had broken the hinges off the previous day, so his visitor had very little trouble moving it aside. He was a Little Person with a blue beard tucked into a golden belt, very bright eyes, about yay tall . . . other things that set him apart from everybody else in Widdle Wearth? I don't know . . . did I mention he was short? Also right now he was angry, but that's just right now, so you mustn't take that as a permanent character trait or some sort of universal thing for . . . people like him.

"Excuse me?" said the Little, otherwise unremarkable Person.

"I'm sorry," stammered Billy. "I just . . . I mean, I was expecting a——"

"White man?"

"Yes! Noooo. No. A wizard. Like a big, tall, impressive . . ."

"Grand?"

"Yes, like a big, Grand Wizard! I mean——" Billy had put his foot firmly in his mouth, which served the double purpose of shutting him up and allowing him to finally eat that last pickled chicken foot he had been saving. Luckily at that moment another Little Person appeared at the door. He looked . . . like the first one. I mean, not exactly alike. I can definitely tell them apart.

"What's the matter, Drawlin?"

"Well, Ballin, it seems our host may not have been expecting people like *us*."

Ballin looked at Billy's panicked face and sighed. "We've talked about this, Drawlin. He's just a product of a literary tradition that has systematically reduced the idea of a racial other to a fantastic, categorical enemy."

"All I'm saying is, it wasn't the system that locked the door as soon as he saw who was knocking." The two Little People stepped inside and made their way to the dining room as they continued this discussion, which is a totally worthwhile dialogue to have and I'm not switching focus just because I'm uncomfortable. Billy swallowed his foot and watched them walk away, completely at a loss over what to do and whether or not to ask if his two guests were related.* He was about to slip out the door and give up on this hole entirely when another set of visitors appeared in his way. These two were clearly brothers.

"What can I do for you, my regular-colored Little People?" he said, with visible relief.

"Fili at your service!" said the one. Nothing, said the other one, because he was a kiwi, an indigenous flightless bird of New Zealand.

---

* In fact, they were brothers. Like, genetically. I promise; I checked.

"At yours and your family's!" replied Billy, remembering his Anglo-Saxon manners this time.

"Drawlin and Ballin are here already, I see," said Fili. "Let us join the gang!"

"Gang?" thought Billy as he speed-dialed the police and then hung up because he didn't want to be that guy. However, he was also upset about what the additional number of visitors implied. "I'm sure there won't be any more of them," he said out loud and, satisfied that this statement would not be comically undercut in a few seconds, he put his door back up and turned to join the Little People—when, *ding-dongs-ho-hos-twinkies,* his bell rang again.

"Sounds like four more," said Fili. "Besides, I saw them coming along behind us in the distance. I have keen eyesight."

"I am a Southern Brown Kiwi," implied the kiwi.

It was not four after all; it was five! Billy had hardly stopped wondering if kiwis were edible before all five of them were inside. Whorey, Slorey, and Kourtney were the names of the first three, all sisters, and Billy was immediately both aroused by them and angry at them for existing. Loin and Groin were the second two, and oh boy, if you think their names are funny, just wait until they say something really sexual. Many a Widdle Wearth song tells of an ancient prophecy that one day, these two Little People will say the funniest, most sexual thing of all time.

"Hello," said Loin and Groin. That wasn't it.

Loin, Groin, Whorey, Slorey, Kourtney, and Whorey, Slorey, and Kourtney's camera crew all made their way to Billy's dining room, which he had luckily just expanded into his snacking parlor so there was ample room for the growing party. "Well, at least there's not five more of them," thought

Billy, and he was about to stride confidently away when there was a massive *thud* on the door. He opened it to find Dumbledalf standing there with four more Little People, one of whom was prostrate, crumpled up on the stoop.

"See, I told you!" said Dumbledalf to the unconscious Little Person. "If you just believe and run straight at the platform, you'll pass right through. Hello, Hairy! Let me introduce Beefer," a shiny Little Person flexed his triceps, "Buffer," a veiny Little Person punched Billy in the stomach, "Aaron Sorkinshield," a self-important Little Person did a line of happy sugar, "and especially Doc!" Doc continued to be unconscious, so they left him on the stoop and joined the rest of the Little People at the table.

The Little People had managed to find the food that Billy had carefully hidden everywhere in plain sight, and they were making a regular party out of it. Aaron Sorkinshield offered some of his special writing powder to everyone, but Whorey, Slorey, and Kourtney promised him that they were already "dancin' with Miley." Beefer and Buffer focused on leaner meats because they knew that the simple carbs in Billy's cake bread would make their body especially receptive to storing fats, and the kiwi located insects and simple invertebrates underground using his highly developed sense of smell. All parties present pretended not to notice the bird feeder in the corner, or the terrible stench everywhere else. Billy was completely overwhelmed, but Dumbledalf, sitting at the head of the table, was wonderfully amused.

"Music!" he called out. "And ghosts! Where are all my ghost friends?" As he began lighting sticks of butter on fire and trying to make them float, the Little People fulfilled his first request with a traditional song of feasting:

Show up a half hour late,
Demand your food be gluten free!
That's what everybody hates,
When you're a guest at their party!

Tell a bunch of inside jokes,
That only half the people get!
Say you'd pay but you're too broke,
That'll make your poor host fret!

So show up a half hour late,
Because that's what everybody hates!

And of course they did none of these dreadful things, because they didn't totally suck as people. Soon, however, the skies grew dark, and Doc finally wandered in from the stoop with a concussion and an acoustic guitar. Doc did kind of suck as a person, so he began to play, and everybody at the party was forced to listen to his mediocre strumming. When it became clear that he wasn't going to stop anytime soon, the Little People made the best of it and sang a deeply meaningful song of ancient loss and profound pain:

Because maybe, you're gonna be the one that saves me,
And after all, you're my wonderwall.
Said maybe (maybe),
You're gonna be the one that saves me (saves me).

As they sang, the wobbit felt the magic of nineties Britpop moving through him, a plaintive and nostalgic sort of magic that bonded everyone in Widdle Wearth together. Then something Gram-ish woke up inside him, and he wished to go see the great mountains, and apply just the right filter to them, and then spend the next thirty to forty minutes trying to find enough service for the page to load so he could see whether or not people he had met once or twice were appreciating just how much he was appreciating the simple beauty of the natural world. Suddenly the microwave let out a great beep, and his nightly ground beef pie with Pop-Tart crust was ready, and very quickly he was once again plain Billy Bagboy with a rumble in his stomach and a family history of Apathetic Heart syndrome.

"Hush," said Dumbledalf, as Doc's head trauma caught up to him and he began to punch the guitar with his fist. "Let Sorkinshield speak!" And this was Sorkinshield's cold open:

"A poet once rhymed: as if it matters how a man is toppled. And seen. Well, if you want to stand on your toes and call yourselves giants, take advantage of the first amendment. Ask yourself this: Do I have the Yahweh disease? It's not the greatest Wearth in the world, sensei. That's what I say. Child, this is war country. You have some of my focus—you have the least proportion, a depressing callback to the time when two great Wearths raced each other into Wspace. We reached for the ceiling, acted like people, we aspired to the opposite of stupidity, we didn't do the opposite of enlarge it, it didn't make us feel the opposite of ferior, as we did in the time when our looking organs looked toward the Wheavens and, with super-extended phalanges, we touched the face of Buddha. Let me say a thing. You want to know a fact? You know what's pretty neat? *I am Gawd. You can't grasp the facts. A trillion yen is pretty neat.*"

This was Sorkinshield's veritable style. He was, if nothing

else, an important Little Person. If he had been allowed, he would probably have gone on like this until he was out of breath, without properly inventing any new characters since the early 2000s. But he was rudely interrupted. Poor Billy couldn't bear it any longer, and he began to feel a shriek coming up inside him. "Sometimes there are flaws in the way you write female characters!" he called out over and over again as he wobbled to the floor; and that was all they could get out of him for a good long while indeed. They were concerned it might be a seizure, but Doc assured them that it was only a *diabetic* seizure, and that his professional medical opinion was to leave the wobbit well enough alone. So they rolled Billy into his diabetic seizure nook and left him well enough alone, forgetting for a moment that Doc had suffered a moderate to severe brain injury and was therefore giving his professional medical opinion based solely on context clues rather than professional medical training of any sort.

"Excitable little fellow," said Dumbledalf. "And why am I surrounded by tiny half-giants? Did I do centaur drugs in the Forbidden Forest again?"

"Excitable is one word for it," said Groin, as everyone in the room waited eagerly for his hilarious sexual punch line, "but I think it's far more accurate to conclude that this wobbit is neither physically nor mentally fit to help us fulfill our quest." They all leaned back, recognizing that this was a valid insight into their situation, but were still disappointed that he hadn't mentioned genitals. "In fact, he looks more like a grocer than a burglar!"

"I am not a groper!" Billy protested as he stumbled back into the room.

"I said grocer."

"Oh. I am definitely a grocer."

The whole party groaned at this. "A grocer?!" howled Beefer and Buffer in disproportionate rage. "A job?!" whined Whorey, Slorey, and Kourtney in genuine befuddlement. "The kiwi is nocturnal?!" is an exclamation you might make were you to study the kiwi's sleep patterns. Finally Dumbledalf would stand it no longer.

"Quiet!" he said, and the whole room fell silent. Slowly and solemnly, he rose from his seat and picked up the honey-honey baked ham from the middle of the table. He placed the meat on Billy's head, then watched the confused wobbit with rapt attention. Finally someone sneezed and Dumbledalf clapped his hands in delight. "The sorting ham has spoken! We have our burglar!"

No one could argue with this, because no one really understood what had happened. Plus, Billy had the traditional lightning-bolt mark on his door, which everyone in Widdle Wearth knew meant either *Burglar looking for work* or *Kite-flying aficionado looking for his keys*. So before Billy could get over the shock of being betrayed by a meat he had so much respect for, Dumbledalf laid out a map and Sorkinshield began laying out the entire exposition. As you can guess, this speech took many hours, and used many stirring invocations, and made everyone feel more intelligent just to have heard it and understood most of it. But in the end, it boiled down to this:

"[Your name is Puff the Magic Dragon. You took my mountain. Prepare to die.]"

As Sorkinshield's speech drew to a close and the swelling violin underscoring faded out, everyone agreed that it truly felt like the end of an episode. So they each trudged, hopped, and seizured to bed, leaving for later the small matters of how to get to the Mountain with Zero Friends, and how to find the side door into it, and who would get to control the playlist on the way. For his part, Billy had begun to realize just how similar questing might be to jogging and would have slept fitfully were it not for the five pounds of fudge he had eaten over the course of Sorkinshield's speech. As he passed out with his head in the refrigerator, he could hear Sorkinshield still humming to himself in the bedroom next to him:

Some day you will find me,
Caught beneath the landslide,
In a champagne supernova,
Champagne supernova in the sky.

Meanwhile, in the hole next door, Billy's extremely well-qualified burglar neighbor finally took the "I Am a Well-Qualified Burglar" sign off his door and shuffled off to bed, resigning himself to yet another season of unemployment. In the hole next to that, Saddam Hussein changed out of his dirty white T-shirt into tomorrow's dirty white T-shirt, content with the knowledge that no one would ever find him in his underground paradise.

II

/r/oastmutton

Billy awoke from his slumber as he always did: with acute chest pain and choking on his own drool. This time, however, it was not drool being forced down Billy's throat.

"Drink your copyjuice, Hairy," Dumbledalf said, squeezing a Capri Sun into Billy's mouth. "Then we can go to summer camp and get Mom and Dad back together."

"My parents are dead!"* sputtered Billy.

"I know," whispered Dumbledalf as a somber look fell suddenly across his face. "I put them in my mirror."

As the deflated wizard went off to cheer himself up by folding his Capri Sun into a tiny cell phone, Billy prepared to roll himself out of his bed and into his waffle lab. What he rolled

---

* Killed by a joint heart attack when they were thirty-five years old (a ripe old age for wobbits). Heart attacks are contagious for wobbits in much the same way yawns are for us.

off of, however, was not a bed, and what he rolled into was certainly nothing like one of Billy's classic pepperoni waffles.*

"Well, look at that! The racist is finally awake," said Drawlin, lifting Billy out of the manure and placing him atop the pony that had produced it. "Now get in touch with your privilege and show us a little canter."

As he took the reins, Billy struggled to keep pace with the rest of the crew. His pony seemed to be straining mightily and looked back at him every so often with the pony equivalent of exasperation. Billy misinterpreted this as hunger and, after licking the pony a few times to see if he might kill two birds with one meal, decided to ask the rest of the party. "Might we stop and get something to eat before we reach the Forest of Metaphorical Importance?" he pleaded. Beefer and Buffer laughed heartily at his suggestion. "Looks like somebody forgot his egg whites and supplemental amino acid complex this morning," jeered Beefer, and Buffer punched Billy in the face to accentuate the point. Billy's spirit and nose broken, he mentioned food no more for the next several minutes. "Besides," he thought, "being hungry and miserable is what a YOLO is all about. Let me not again forget."†

Once the crew had thoroughly left Wobbottabad behind, they stopped in a valley with a nearby stream to rest one final time before they entered the forest. Everyone dismounted,

---

* Billy's classic pepperoni waffles were so popular in Wobbottabad that they've single-handedly caused the choking deaths of twenty-three wobbits. If I may hold you in confidence, dear reader, the secret to the recipe is that you place the pepperonis under the waffles. And inside them. And on top of them. Then you boil the rest of the pepperoni into a syrup for drinking later.

† He would. See pages 18, 27, 28, 67, 73, 84, 113, 124, 126, and all the other ones.

and it was then they noticed that Dumbledalf had never come back from the game of Hide-n-Leave-for-a-Couple-Days they had played on the road to pass the time. This concerned Aaron Sorkinshield very much, especially because just before he disappeared, he had seen Dumbledalf poking an earthworm and muttering to himself that all the secrets must have gotten loose again.

Thankfully, these worries did not faze some of the more carefree Little People. Whorey, Slorey, and Kourtney, for example, stayed busy uploading selfies of themselves frolicking on the grass, and the paparazzi, springing out of the ground like dandelions, snapped pictures of the girls snapping pictures of themselves. The flashing of the camera bulbs amused Kiwi, annoyed Fili, and set Doc into an epileptic fit that everyone else laughed off. Ballin and Drawlin fell into a debate about the politics of respectability and the implications of Whorey's relationship with their cousin Kayenne, a bona-fide hero of Southside Widdle Wearth known for his fiery outbursts. Beefer and Buffer bench-pressed the ponies while Billy closed his eyes and tried to imagine that YOLOs were no more threatening than his usual breakfast cereal: sugary and delicious grizzly bear cooked with chocolate milk and maybe a little bacon grease.*

Billy was jolted out of this silent reverie by the abrupt appearance of Sorkinshield next to him.

"Have you signed the thing?"

"The thing?"

"It's nothing."

"The thing is nothing?"

---

* Have you ever cooked a grizzly bear? They aren't half as revolting as you'd think, though killing one is twice as illegal as you'd want.

"The contract is nothing."

"Wait. What's the contract?"

"The contract's the thing."

"The thing that you need me to sign?"

"That's the thing."

Sorkinshield turned off sharply to the right, and Billy found himself holding a small stack of paper in his hands. These were the conditions of his employment, and they went like this:

All aforementioned treasure, including all Academy Awards, Golden Globes, Kids' Choice Awards, enthusiastic Rolling Stone *reviews, and any other valuables are, upon discovery, declared sole property of AARON SORKINSHIELD to be distributed at his discretion. Any withholding, burglary, or unintentional "failing to mention" of any such treasure by BILLY BAGBOY will result in immediate expulsion from the party, forfeit of any and all profit earned, and an extremely long monologue, an excerpt of which is below.*

The monologue that followed was extensive and cruel, but it was also bitingly clever with plenty of quotable material suitable for posters or GIF sets. Unfortunately, Billy was more or less illiterate, as wobbits consider being able to read a rather dangerous step on the road to being able to read nutrition facts.* He was, however, very pleased to see "Billy Bagboy" written in such big impressive letters and tore out the bits that contained his name while feeding the rest to his pony.

---

* Once, when our Billy was but eight years old, he came much too close to reading the words "Sugar: 3600g" on his sixty-pack of Fruit Roll-Ups. In the nick of time, he choked on the five Fruit Roll-Ups in his mouth, depriving him of enough oxygen that it killed the one brain cell that was still trying up there.

After one more check of their supplies and one last holler of "Olly, olly, oxen free!" in the hopes of drawing out Dumbledalf, the crew set out to travel through the night, more than a bit discouraged by the disappearance of the one person who had any real abilities.* The rowdy band journeyed far as the sun grew low. They passed through the Loan Lands, where the people had been crushed by massive, inescapable graduate school debt and took to eating their degrees before eating one another. They passed the Jersey Shore, Beverly Hills, and other wicked places that goodness dare not touch. They told many a joke and riddle to lighten the mood as the weather worsened and the sky grew dark. Kiwi told a particularly hilarious and clever one that had the whole group laughing for almost an hour, though the bird had intended it as a mating call.

Alas, there was more misery than laughter that night. Kiwi accidentally pecked the neck of his pony, and the poor beast was so frightened that it jumped into the river and drowned, taking a good portion of the supplies with it.† The rain that came down chilled the Little People and the poor wobbit so terribly that they were forced to stop their trek through the deep dark Forest of Metaphorical Importance almost immediately.‡ They set up camp near the forest's edge, with Whorey whining about her ruined hair and Ballin accusing Sorkinshield

---

* A sample of Dumbledalf's many abilities: sleeping with his eyes open, coughing up doves, and forgetting how not to fly.

† Never ford the river.

‡ As Drawlin later noted, the pit stop was like a beautiful sunset, giving comfort before the long, dark night. Because it was *like* this phenomenon but could not be exactly equated with this phenomenon, the edge of the forest was more emblematic of a simile than a metaphor in their travels.

of redlining their campsite. It was then that Fili's keen eyes spotted a faint white-blue glow far off through the trees.

"What could it be?" queried Sorkinshield, as he quickly began brainstorming thematic points the faint light could hammer home. All of the Little People put forward their best guesses. Perhaps it was the camp of some nonthreatening creatures, like the Orcs-Who-Don't-Appear-in-This-Book or film critics. Perhaps it was a spotlight, destined to shine on Whorey, Slorey, and Kourtney so they could film their new slow-paced reality show, *Slorey and Kourtney Take a Dramamine*. But Sorkinshield was sure it was a deadly enemy and did not want to risk any of them running into more trouble. That is, until he noticed the shivering wobbit standing completely stationary behind a tree.

"Billy, my Bagboy. The time has come for you to truly YOLO," Sorkinshield said. "I suggest you pick up a weapon and stand a post. Either way, I don't give a damn what you think you are entitled to."

"I get a weapon?" asked Billy.

"Oh no, that's just an expression. Your incredible burgling skills that you've shown no evidence of so far will surely suffice. Am I mistaken?" Aaron looked at the rest of his crew for support. They were called supporting actors for a reason. All nodded vigorously and added murmurs of "Oh yes, surely it is just a few film critics," and "I'd go myself, Billy, but I have recently become blind."

So with that, Billy Bagboy set off up over the river and through the woods to check it out by himself. "Atta boy, Billy! If you run into anything dangerous, just scream like a scared little fat man," Sorkinshield called after him.

Wandering up the hill amongst the trees, Billy approached the white-blue glow. He stumbled and made quite the commotion, being not all that used to moving, but the glow never went out or faded, and was soon joined by a manic clicking. It was like the chorus of a hundred beetles wearing tap shoes and trying unsuccessfully to choreograph a routine to "Who Let the Balrogs Out?"* The sound made Billy dizzy. Soon, though, he was right outside the clearing. He peered in and clutched his neck fat in horror.

Trolls. Big and pimply, a group of trolls sat in front of various computer screens, typing away, using all their fingers at once.† They stopped only to giggle maliciously to themselves or open a new tab. Sweat poured from their pale brows, and their swivel chairs, black and filthy, swayed with menace. Trolls such as these never venture into the daylight. Their backs are permanently hunched, their mouths thin and twisted into the most horrifying of grins. Billy had never encountered anything so terrible in his entire life, and he had just spent all day with Whorey, Slorey, and Kourtney. Not to mention the smell. Oh, the stench that wafted through that space was enough to make even the wobbit lose his appetite and stop trying to eat one of the wheels of the swivel chairs.

Billy covered his nose and weighed his options. He could

---

* Later in the forest, the sound would be exactly that, but because you cannot fairly compare a thing to itself, it still did not qualify as a metaphor. While the overall forest reeked of metaphorical importance, our weary travelers began to wonder if perhaps the things inside the forest were just things inside a forest.

† This impressed Billy a great deal, since wobbit fingers are usually so covered in oils or syrups that they stick to one another, making wobbit hands more like mitts, which they then clumsily smash on keyboards when ordering calzones online.

go back to warn the others. He could see if he could use their Wi-Fi to check his email. But before the wobbit could formulate a proper plan, one of the trolls up and spoke.

"Creepshots is back up," said the troll, prompting murmurs of approval from the others as they intensified the speed of their typing.

"What else rhymes with wetback?" mused a second troll who was now scrolling down an infinitely long page with his curled fingernails. "How about lazy wetback?"

"That's offensive!" blurted out Billy, unable to contain himself. Suddenly he was drawn in by the trolls' magic. Under their spell, he walked forward until he was out in the open, the leering trolls right before him.*

"Well, if it isn't the PC police, come to demonstrate how the New World Order Shadow Government wants to squash all original thought," said the first troll. The others looked up and stared at Billy with their yellow eyes.

"No!" cried Billy, knowing he should ignore them but finding it impossible. "My name is Billy—"

"Billy Bagboy of Wobbottabad. Mother's maiden name is Gram and social security number is 391-87-5432," read a troll off his jailbroken smart phone screen. "I just enrolled you as a member of the Communist party and used your savings account to ship four thousand pounds of cotton candy to the UN."

As Billy stammered helplessly, the first troll puffed up his chest and introduced himself. "I am L33tB33tr. King of the

---

* Billy was very good at recognizing racism in others, and less good at recognizing it in himself. In his defense, though, it is very hard to recognize anything inside a wobbit.

subreddit for hentai involving one or more deep sea creatures," said the first troll. His face, illuminated by the computer screen, was plump and ever so slightly green.

The second troll swiveled around to face Billy as well. "I
am IllumiNazi, overlord of the land of YouTube comments," he
said and smiled, revealing a row of teeth shaped like swastikas.

"And I am BarromneyOsama," pronounced the third,
"Mayor of Area Fifty-one on Foursquare."

Billy found himself very angry. Furious, in fact. More furious than he had been when his manager at the grocery store
had started selling produce. Madder even than when he'd accidentally taken a bite of a tomato, thinking it was some sort of
giant Fruit Gusher. His very soul demanded that he know the
real names of these vile creatures.

"Reveal yourselves!" he screamed. The third troll turned
around, yet said nothing. His teeth, shaped like butts, gleamed
in the computer screen light. "How can you possibly think
Jesus was a Reptilian?" Billy yelled again. The troll did not
respond, but began collating GIFs of Harmony Korine's early
films. Billy approached the massive creature but could not
bring himself to lay a hand on him. His skin seemed to shim-
mer in the firelight. It was like the troll was not really there
at all.

Under the river and around the wood, the Little People
heard Billy's screams. At first, they resolved to ignore them
and go back to sleep, but Kourtney thought that maybe if
Billy had lived long enough to scream not once, but twice, the
enemy must not be so threatening. "In any case," she said, "you
guys are boring me. I did not sign a contract allowing people
to watch me sleep on a webcam every night just to sleep on
the ground with a bunch of losers." So she started up the hill

and, after much thought and a couple of minor strokes suffered by Doc, the rest of the crew followed.

"You're a coward!" Billy screamed at the troll. The troll, now satisfied with his outrage, turned to face the tiny wobbit. "That may be true," he said, "but you're a grocer who has no business being on a YOLO in the first place. Also, Jon Stewart is a war criminal."

Billy's anger immediately faded and a dark, soul-crushing depression seeped into him like water rushing into a gorge.* "The troll is right," thought Billy. "I'm not fit for a YOLO. I'm not fit for anything. No one cares for me. I was sent up here by my own crew to die. They'd be better off without me."

"So why don't you just get on with it then?" said L33tB33tr, reading Billy's mind by designing an algorithm to analyze and predict his future Google searches. Billy sniffled.

The third troll gestured to flames and tossed Billy some rope and a large spit. Billy wept as he sat down on the ground and began to tie himself up. "It's better this way," thought Billy. He put a gag in his mouth and tied his hands together tightly. "I will YOLO no more."

By the time Billy had finished tying himself up, the Little People were gathered around the trolls' clearing. "Trolls!" whispered Sorkinshield to his frightened crew. "What an unexpected twist."

"Ah, Aaron Sorkinshield!" yelled L33tB33tr into the night. "The famed adventurer. Leader of the *Studio 60 on the Silmarillion Strip* quest. Or should I say, the *canceled* quest."†

---

* Again, simile. It's like this forest isn't even trying.

† This much-anticipated quest met an unfortunate end when the entire party was buried alive in an avalanche of exactly 30 rocks.

Sorkinshield's blood boiled and, before anyone could stop him, he stepped out into the open. "How dare you!" he shouted at the trolls, who swiveled to greet him as Billy cried and wordlessly marinated himself in a variety of nearby herbs and spices.

"You should be lucky we even know your name, which wouldn't be the case if you hadn't sold out to be the sycophantic scribe of Silly Cone Valley," taunted IllumiNazi.* Though Sorkinshield's will was strong and the Little People hidden behind him begged him to ignore the trolls' harsh words, he was soon just as depressed and deliciously seasoned as Billy.

One by one, the trolls targeted the Little People hiding behind the trees, drawing them out with slurs and taunts. They lamented Whorey's lack of talent and Slorey's lack of fame. They mocked Kourtney for being entirely irrelevant and easily the dumbest of the bunch. They told Ballin and Drawlin that their parents should have been on food stamps, and told Doc he shouldn't have eaten all those stamps for food. They said Beefer and Buffer were overcompensating and argued to Loin and Groin that schoolteachers were overly compensated. One by one, each was so demoralized they tied themselves to a spit, ready to be roasted and eaten.

As the ravenous BarromneyOsama began to place them over the fire, IllumiNazi let out a terrified scream.

"What?" asked Barromney, dropping Doc on the ground.

"It's my subreddit," answered IllumiNazi. "Somebody is totally mixing up Whedonverse mythologies!"

"Impossible!" yelled L33tB33tr. "Don't they know how

---

* A valley where a bunch of young people design very silly cones, which other young people buy for lots of money until an even sillier cone comes out.

much *Firefly* means to Joss?" They gathered around IllumiNazi's computer and stared in wonder as the screen whirred and changed before them. They trolled furiously, but whoever was on the other side was making just as little sense as any of them.

Without warning, Dumbledalf burst into the clearing, iPad in hand, muttering incantations over it. "God, I hate Safari. Can anyone tell me how to clear my search history?" he yelled, oblivious to the fact that his friends were tied up over scorching flames.

"Are you WashintonWizard2?" accused L33tB33tr. Dumbledalf ignored him and went right back to his iPad magic. The screen whizzed and buzzed. The trolls frantically tried to regain control of their forums and message boards but it was too late. They were doomed from the instant Dumbledalf failed to correctly copy the URL for a cat meme and instead lambasted them with the Wikipedia page for erectile dysfunction. Yet trolls being trolls, they refused to give up.* They worked through the night trying to take back their message boards, losing an entire two hours to Dumbledalf mistaking Facebook's search bar for the "What's on your mind?" update option. Before they knew it, morning came, and with it, the sun. The natural sunlight was so shocking to the trolls' introverted nervous systems that they all fell dead on the spot. They had been pwned, and pwned good.

Then Dumbledalf tripped on a wire and the computer screens burst into flames, destroying all evidence of the encounter. It was a clean kill, and the online community would attribute their deaths to Anonymous for years to come.

---

* Ironically, it is this same quality that will make our poor wobbit so endearing in the chapters to come.

Thus, the trolls' spell was broken. Billy and the Little People again remembered their reasons to live.* They untied themselves, grabbed a number of potentially very important swords that were lying on the ground, and circled around Dumbledalf, eager for answers.

"How did you know where to find us? How did you know how to defeat the trolls? And where did you go in the first place?"

But Sorkinshield quickly pushed to the forefront and silenced the group's clamoring. "Enough questions," he said. "From now on I have one answer for you, and one answer only: Let Dumbledalf be Dumbledalf."

"Who's Dumbledalf?" asked Dumbledalf. Then he set his hat on fire and tossed it into the wind, grumbling that the stupid old bird never did anything for itself nowadays.

---

* Food.

III

A Short but Very Expensive Rest

The wobbit was solemn on the day following his narrow escape from the trolls. He barely touched the duck in his second turducken cheeseburger and was convinced he had caught a glimpse of his feet when he'd woken up that morning, causing him to lose his appetite all the more.

The rest of the band was also out of tune. Dumbledalf mistook his staff for a potions master, and wouldn't stop talking to it until it promised to kill him when the time was right; Sorkinshield lectured less frequently, but still frequently enough to convey the social injustices of the Widdle Wearth media; and Beefer and Buffer only completed reps of three-quarter squats, not even mustering enough energy to go down to parallel.

There was a stench of evil lurking around every corner, and no amount of Dumbledalf's ninety-nine-cent Magic Air Fresheners would dispel it. Before long, the ragtag crew came upon a sight that made even Buffer's biceps seem small. Doc ceased whistling for the first time since their YOLO began.

"Is that the Mountain with Zero Friends?" Billy asked.

"No, that's Shaq," corrected Ballin.

Billy apologized profusely to the four-time NBA champion and future Hall of Famer as Drawlin glared at him in disbelief. Ballin gestured higher, to a vast range of peaks in the distance—these were the Mountains Whose Peaks Are Concealed by Gathering Precipitation Around Their Summits. Whorey, Slorey, and Kourtney thought the spectacle was the biggest thing they had ever seen. Loin and Groin silently passed up this opportunity.

The wobbit and his friends would have to travel treacherous roads through the Mountains Whose Peaks Are Concealed by Gathering Precipitation Around Their Summits before entering into a wild wasteland, also known as the Land without a Netflix Password. Only after a harrowing stint through the forest of Jerkwood would the Mountain with Zero Friends be visible.

The thought of the lengthy journey made Billy miss Wobbottabad and his king-size, memory-foam bed with a built-in toilet. He released a sigh of sadness, then ingested a cheese puff of resignation and washed it down with the chocolate milk of burgeoning resolve.

Meanwhile Slorey, who had developed a habit of naming trees and rocks and anything else she took a fancy to as they walked, noticed something strange.

"Dumbledalf," she whined, "this is the third time we've passed Lamar Oakom!"

"And every time he seems to have more and more crack in him," grumbled Drawlin.*

---

* Get it? Because he's a tree.

"Where exactly are we going?"

"To the Old Phony House of L. Ron, and the valley of Livinwell," proclaimed Dumbledalf. "He and his Elf Cult are practitioners of the ancient two-month-old religion of Celebritology. They are always more than willing to take in those who are weary and confused and defenseless. I have sent an owl ahead to notify them of our coming."

In reality, the owl Dumbledalf had sent had only gone a few feet before landing on Doc's head and pecking him for the last twenty minutes, but the travelers pressed on regardless. Livinwell was the last Old Phony House south of the Hills and, despite its large, glowing, neon Celebritology sign, it was not so easy to find. The sun was setting, and the wobbit and friends had yet to arrive at their destination. In Celebritology cosmology, it had been a complete cycle of the three moons of Tatooine.

As they continued on their search for Livinwell, teatime passed, and so did suppertime, and so did all manner of times invented by rich white people with too much time on their hands. Dumbledalf kept turning his Mischief Map this way and that in an attempt to figure out where they were, and his Mischief Map kept remaining an unhelpful and perturbed stick with ants on it. Finally the entire party became so tired and hungry that they were willing to believe anything and trust anybody for even the faintest hope of nourishment and rest. This, of course, was when they found Celebritology.

There it was: a glorious, stark building at the bottom of a beautiful valley, and at the intersection of Ivar and Hollywood Boulevard. Billy never forgot those final steps toward Livinwell. The trees transformed into palms, and he could now faintly detect the smell of expensive cologne, Louis Vuitton, and the constant need for approval.

"Oh god, it smells like veganism!" thought Billy. He looked up at the stars, and then he looked down and saw stars all around him. The ones in the sky were burning bright and glorious; the ones around him were just tan. Then there came a rush of song emerging from the windows of Porsches passing by:

> O! Look at us singing,
> Our diamonds are blinging!
> Grammys we're winning,
> And Botox beginning!
> O! Tra-la-la-lally!
> The golden hills of Cali*!

> O! Why are you staring?
> Is our beauty that glaring?
> Okay, yes it is, feel free to keep staring,
> That's Versace we're wearing!
> Tril-lil-lil-lolly!
> One more Emmy! Gee, golly!

> O! My personal trainer I'm phoning,
> Who keeps my muscles growing!
> More honing, more toning,
> Then fake bronzing I'm going!
> Come, wobbit and friends,
> Makeover time!
> It won't cost a dime!
> Although, to be fair, I'm not fluent in dimes.

---

* How people who are not from California refer to California.

O! First we'll go playing,
Then to space-gods praying,
Don't be nervous we're famous,
Or that our church is from Uranus,
Just join in on our ways,
And give in to the daze!
And every day we thank L. Ron,
We're not stuck doing plays!

So they giggled and sang in their Porsches, and pretty fair nonsense I daresay you think it. Not that they would care; they only cared for sense and sensibility if it might land them a nomination, and only examined their pride or prejudice if it might cost them an endorsement deal.

"What funny clothes!" said one Celebritologist as he stepped out of his Porsche with two Elf Cult escorts on each arm. "Did you get them off the sale rack at Rural Outfitters?" The escorts giggled in unison.

Despite the offensiveness of the Celebritologist's comment, the wobbit and friends looked past his rudeness and into his magnificent complexion and ridiculous good looks. Whorey, Slorey, and Kourtney were especially flustered: waving, smiling, and attempting to have his celebrity children all at once. He laughed and made love to them and sent them on their way as the band of friends crossed a very short crosswalk and finally came to the last Old Phony House. When they drew close, its glass doors slid wide open, as if by some magic, and then closed again if they walked too far away from the sensors. Evil things did not come into the valley of Livinwell, or at least they never made it all the way there before getting fed up with the traffic and just settling down in Long Beach instead.

The master of the house, L. Ron, was one of those people who came into strange stories before the beginning of history; even before the great Klingon battle of the ninth century, and the death of Molor by the Sword of Kahless. In his early years, L. Ron may have started out as a mere pulp-fiction writer of Widdle Wearth lore, but he became so much more. He became friends with a select group of individuals.

He was as wise as Spock and as powerful as the Force. He was politically savvy enough to command the Battlestar *Galactica* and respectable enough to completely avoid *The Big Bang Theory*. He made countless appearances on *The Twilight Zone* as the surprise twist ending, and he is the only man to win first place at the *Planet of the Apes* costume contest without wearing a costume. L. Ron doesn't always drink beer, but when he does, he drinks Buzz Lightbeer.

He was initially hesitant to welcome the visitors, professing a belief in what he called "self-help." He had hoped the wobbit and his friends would figure out their own problems by analyzing the meaning of their humanoid thoughts. However, after realizing that the group could not craft beds and shelter with their minds, and that spiritual enlightenment would not keep them from starving to death, he gave up and simply helped them.

L. Ron gave his visitors brand-new robes, which looked suspiciously like bargain-rack Jedi cloaks. The Celebritology center also accommodated them with spa services and complimentary margaritas, and, on weekends, arranged marriages. When Billy and the Little People learned that "complimentary" in this case meant "you should take it as a compliment that I think you can afford this," they were a little disappointed in the class warfare, but nonetheless forgave L. Ron because they were already drunk and feeling extremely relaxed.

At the end of a two-week relaxation cycle, each member of the crew received a bill in their hotel suite for five thousand silver pennies. Billy, Dumbledalf, and the Little People had never seen that much money in their lives, except for Whorey, Slorey, and Kourtney, who had almost that exact sum tucked away in their bras for emergencies and extra support. They reluctantly paid, but were thrilled to learn that this meant they had evolved to the next level of celebrity status. Sorkinshield gave himself a pat on the back and took all the credit.

To describe the importance of this promotion, L. Ron called on the most famous member of the Elf Cult of Celebritology: Tóm Crúìsëanór. He slid onto the scene in a dress shirt and tighty-whities, having just finished rubbing his naked body on an ottoman for three hours. Billy and the Little People were speechless—not because Tóm Crúìsëanór was the most famous Elf Cult celebrity in all of Widdle Wearth, but because in person he was only two feet tall. Whorey, Slorey, and Kourtney had barely begun telling Crúìsëanór what big fans they were when he interrupted and dramatically proclaimed, "You had me at hello!"

He had never acquired the skill of paying attention to people past the first word they said to him, but for some reason every time he tried to tell them this, they gasped and applauded. The sisters were no exception, as Whorey squealed with excitement, Slorey passed out, and Kourtney became visibly aroused.

"Congratulations on evolving to the next level of celebrity status," Crúìsëanór informed them, reading from his script. "By staying here at Livinwell, paying five thousand silver pennies, and exhibiting the inherent qualities of potential stardom, you have already achieved the level of I Think I

Recognize That Person from Somewhere celebrity. The road to the status of Universal, God-Man Popularity like mine is only a few short weeks and several million dollars away."

Tóm Crúìsëanór then went on to explain the eight levels of Celebritology while running back and forth across the room and defusing a bomb he had set:

Level 1: Poor Person (1 or 2 silver pennies)

Level 2: I Think I Recognize That Person from Somewhere (5,000 silver pennies)

Level 3: I Definitely Recognize That Person from Somewhere (10,000 silver pennies)

Level 4: Oh My God, It's That Guy! (150,000 silver pennies)

Level 5: Child / Reality Star (150,000 silver pennies and a sacrificial tauntaun)

Level 6: B-list Celebrity (500,000 silver pennies and your firstborn child)

Level 7: A-list Celebrity (2,000,000 silver pennies and your first-adopted child)

Level 8: Universal, God-Man Popularity (redacted, but something along the lines of 100,000,000,000,000 pieces of silver, 40 pounds of flesh, and Leah Remini's soul trapped inside a Living Dolls blooper reel)

If they were to make it to Universal, God-Man Popularity, Billy and the Little People were told that they would be initiated on board a secret spaceship where only the most popular celebrities gained admittance. The ship was named the *Millennium Falcon,* and it was piloted by none other than Celebritologist Jóhn Trávóltáhrós, who personally gave every passenger a deep tissue massage before they went to bed, whether they wanted it or not.

Billy sensed that perhaps Livinwell was not the place for a wobbit. He was beginning to have body-image issues, which, for a wobbit, meant that he was beginning to see images of his body in mirrors. Sorkinshield felt he wasn't getting the recognition he deserved, and Dumbledalf felt that for once he was not the craziest person in the room. So despite the flirty texts from Jóhn Trávóltáhrós and the blinding smiles from Tóm Crúìsëanór's dreamy lips, they decided that they couldn't stay in Livinwell.

"I feel the need for speed!" Tóm told them.

"You're foaming at the mouth," the Little People replied. "We can't understand you."

Tóm Crúìsëanór departed, disgruntled, with a homemade Academy Award in hand and a strange desire to go kill a psychiatrist and eat his still-beating heart. Only Kiwi seemed impressed. Birds are easily impressed.

Before Billy and his friends left Livinwell, L. Ron requested to see the swords they had brought from the Internet trolls' lair. Of course, he could not tell them much about the weapons upon inspection, as his expertise was in light sabers. These were just regular swords used as Italian sausage cleavers in the Moblin Wars.

He was able to deduce, however, that Sorkinshield's sword was called Porkist—the famous Moblin-skewering sword of old. Dumbledalf's sword was named Hamdring—the meat carver that the King of Fondle'n once wore before being forced out of office by allegations of sexually appropriate behavior in the workplace.

"Whence did the Internet trolls get them? I wonder," said Sorkinshield, looking at his sausage cleaver with new interest.

"I could not say," said L. Ron, "but one may guess that the trolls got them off eBay, or through a Groupon discount. I have also heard whispers of forgotten treasures in the Mines of Mamma Mia since the Little People and the Moblin War."

Sorkinshield pondered these words. "I will keep this sword in honor," he said. "May it soon cleave the Moblins' sausages once again!"

Everyone looked at Loin and Groin, but they were too busy reviving Doc, whom Crúìsëanór had run through with a samurai sword on his way out.

"May I take a gander at your map before you go?" asked L. Ron, as a medical team bandaged Doc and a brainwashing team scrubbed all memory of trauma from his mind.

All of a sudden, as L. Ron gazed at the map, mystical Poon Runes glowed upon the surface, revealing its secret contents. L. Ron was able to read the Poon Runes because, as you know, every member of the *Harvard Lampoon* is guaranteed to become a celebrity, earning automatic admittance to the Elf Cult of Celebritology and, occasionally, a polite hello from B. J. Novak.

"Ah, yes, Poon Runes," said L. Ron. "The writers of the *Harvard Lampoon* invented them so that they could spend a century and a half printing a magazine that's literally unreadable."

"But how do we reveal the secrets of Poon?" asked Whorey unironically.

"In order to see the Poon Runes," said L. Ron, "you have to have drunk the same amount of beer that the members of the *Lampoon* drank when they wrote them. You also have to download the *Harvard Lampoon*'s free iPad app, and follow them on Twitter at www.twitter.com/harvardlampoon."

"*Expellyourarmses!*" Dumbledalf yelled, and he grabbed the map from L. Ron's hands, vexed that the mysterious leader should find this out first. "What says it?" he asked.

L. Ron squinted at the Runes. "It says, 'Watch *Conan*, weeknights on TBS.' "

The wobbit and his friends were not sure of the meaning of this Poon Rune, but one thing was clear: the *Harvard Lampoon* is really, really cool and you should tell your friends that it still exists.

Unused to such short messages, Sorkinshield asked if there was anything else written on the map.

But L. Ron only shrugged. "Just some boring stuff about the exact way you can enter the Mountain with Zero Friends and slay Puff the Magic Dragon. All the other jokes must have been written after additional beers were consumed. Now, that'll be four hundred silver pennies for the free advice."

Their bill finally settled, L. Ron took his leave, requesting, "Beam me up!" to any Celebritologist on the floors above. When there was no answer, he took the elevator.

The next morning was as fresh as any other in the valley of Livinwell: blue skies and never a cloud, until you actually try to go to the beach and then of course it's overcast and windy. The wobbit and his friends rode away amid songs of vanity, with their hearts ready for more adventure and their pockets filled with kale because Kirstié Alléydriel had eaten all the other snacks.* The Mountains Whose Peaks Are Concealed by Gathering Precipitation Around Their Summits lay ahead, and the YOLO had only just begun.

---

* With *Widdle Wearth Wweight Wwatchers*, you too can eat all the snacks and feel good about it.

IV

Overtook in Underwear

There were several paths that led into the mountains, but most were infested with evil creatures, dead ends, and dead creatures that had met a most evil end. By following the sage advice of L. Ron, the wobbit and the Little People were able to choose the correct path upon which to continue their journey. "The universe is how you perceive it," L. Ron had explained. "Move mountains with your mind, not your might. Take the third path on the left."

It had been many days since they had left Livinwell, but still they ventured upward, unable to afford the Express Lane tickets that would have taken them directly to the summit. Soon they were high enough to look out over the lands they had crossed, the convenient attribute of geography that makes a good YOLO so cinematic in the first place. For the first time Billy saw how far they'd traveled: not very far. He had forgotten that Livinwell was only a couple miles away from his wobbit-hole and that most of their time was spent with the Little People waiting up ahead for Billy to wobble faster on his squatty legs. A chain was only as strong as its weakest link, and a traveling expedition was only as fast as its weakest link. He could also see he had left his front door wide open.

The Little People were quiet, and even Whorey, Slorey, and Kourtney had given up on complaining once they realized how hot they looked covered in volcanic ash. The silence was broken only by the sound of water flowing from the ice-capped peaks, reminding them all how much they had to use the bathroom.*

Billy was concerned about the YOLO. Dumbledalf was worried too, noting that the centaurs they were riding seemed to have been horrifically disfigured. The YOLO was in grave danger: at the pace they were going, it might very well have taken more than one lifetime. But a mountain was no place to move quickly, as one wrong step could send a traveler plummeting. A mountain climber falling thousands of feet to his death was nothing remarkable in the area, as the Land of Foolhardy Idiot Mountain Climbers was just down the way. But if one of our merry band was to fall, they'd be left with the remaining dreaded number of thirteen travelers, a big no-no in the YOLO department. Seven-on-seven games of field hockey would henceforth be impossible. Should terrible fate ordain this to happen, all agreed that Doc should kill himself to get it back to an even twelve.

The bleak was only turning bleaker.† Billy implored Dumbledalf to do something to boost morale.

---

* You may be wondering why it is that all these books with all these YOLOs never show anybody, you know, answering Widdle Wearth's call. The answer is quite simple: none of them have gone to the bathroom once since chapter one. This may be a problem later!

† Soon things will be bleakest.

The wizard cleared his throat. "On YOLOs you are to expect the unexpected. As you may expect, this would leave the previously expected unexpected. We can't be expected to expect both the expected and unexpected."

He pulled a broken, entirely unusable bright-pink umbrella from his cloak.

"I'm expecting rain."

With that, the sound of thunder from the east echoed through the mountains.* Billy shivered with fear, which, thanks to the energy-amplifying properties of his fat rolls, shook the entire mountain even more.

Boulders tumbled down from the cliffs, loosened from their centuries-old lodgings by the wobbit-induced rumble. The rocks were almost as difficult to dodge as the raindrops, and a good deal more difficult to swallow.

The band took cover under a hanging boulder, hoping it wouldn't fall and squash them all, rendering the next nine chapters pointless. The wind whipped about and the rain blew sideways into the cave. Loin and Groin began unpacking the food bags.

"Quickly, help us drain the sacks," Loin cried. "We need to rub them out so the wetness doesn't stick." The Little People sighed. Another false alarm.

Kourtney, meanwhile, stepped out from under the rock to find a better Wi-Fi signal, and spotted a light in the distance. She took a picture of it and uploaded it to MaceBook.† Upon

---

* Thunderstorms from the east are loud, violent, and always in a hurry to get where they're going. Western storms, on the other hand, are pretty chill.

† A social networking site for bloodthirsty warriors. Dumbledalf claimed to have had a role in starting it, but Sorkinshield reminded him that if he had invented MaceBook, he would have invented MaceBook.

receiving the notification, Dumbledalf decided it was best that they move toward the light, as it might be the golden bitch, a pesky female golden retriever he had been trying to get his hands on for years.

Billy looked upon the light with wonder. He believed in the gold light, the orgastic future that year by year recedes before us. It eluded him then, but that's no matter—tomorrow he would would run faster, stretch out his arms farther . . . and then one fine morning—well, that actually seems like a lot to expect from a wobbit. He quietly adjusted his aspirations and ate an entire carton of Stephen Colbert's AmeriCone Dream, spoon against the caramel, borne back ceaselessly into the ice cream cramps.

Billy wobbled out into the howling storm and was immediately struck by a boulder, which ricocheted off his right love handle and out into the abyss below. It came from the rock giants, three towering forces as tall as mountains and made of the same thing mountains are made of. They were essentially mountains.

To reach the light in the distance, the YOLOers had to traverse a narrow ridge. On the right were the giants and the tumbling boulders that threatened to knock them to their deaths. On the left was a deep crevice full of diamonds, re-inforced concrete, and steel beams. They were truly stuck between a *rock* and a *hard place*.[*]

"Let's go again," said one giant. "On three. Rock, paper, scissors, shoot!"

"Are we throwing on 'scissors' or 'shoot' this time?"

---

[*] Copyright 2013, *The Harvard Lampoon*.

"We've been playing this game for centuries, Dave. You know we go on shoot."

After four hundred years, the other two rock giants were rather sick of Dave's mind games.

They each raised a fist. "Rock, paper, scissors, shoot!"

They all threw rock. It was their millionth tie in a row. The mountain climber that they had imprisoned as scorekeeper put up his "One Million Ties!" banner and launched some confetti, but it was too small for the giants to see.[*]

The giants yelled in anger at themselves and one another. They kicked and punched the mountainside, sending boulders tumbling down toward the Little People.

"Why don't you idiots ever throw anything other than rock?"

It was classic reverse psychology.

"Why don't *you* throw something other than rock?"

Reverse psychology in reverse.

"Maybe I will. Watch this."

The giants all steadied their hands. "Rock, paper, scissors . . . shoot!"

They all threw rock. Dave's mind games were such BS.

At last our weary travelers arrived at a landing safe from the giants' wrath. They could now see the light was a pink-and-yellow neon sign—an arrow pointing to the entrance of a cave. The words "No Evil Beasts Here" blinked on and off,

---

[*] The scorekeeper was a sad sort, of course, having been imprisoned most of his life. He had but one dream: to one day write a musical about Rock Paper Scissors that college students could perform for free to one another. Sadly, musicals had yet to be invented in Widdle Wearth, and besides, can you imagine what that musical would be like? There would have to be songs in it.

connected to one of the longest power cords in the land. As a precaution, Sorkinshield checked his phone, but the cave proved to have a five-star rating on Welp.* "Not the most ideal location," noted the top comment, "but what this cave lacks in amenities it definitely makes up for in no evil beasts."

Billy was wary of the cave. It was difficult to discern how far back it went, and whether or not it finally had some sort of toilet in it. But the rest of the company had already begun to unpack, and Dumbledalf was busy ordering a stalagmite in the corner to not be a Voldemancer anymore.

They laid out their wet clothing and reclined in their underwear. (Wobbits wore boxers, Little People preferred briefs, and wizards lacked genitals.) Before long everyone was asleep save Billy. This hole-in-the-mountain was a far cry from his hole-in-the-ground, and he had peculiar dreams about the back of the cave sliding open to reveal an old-fashioned diner filled with Italian clientele plotting their enemies' downfalls and having rather conservative ideas about gender. Billy lay frozen as one of the waiters walked out the door, flipped off the light switch for the neon arrow, and hung a new sign which read "Moblin Cave: Grand Opening!"

The waiter grabbed the ponies and led them into the eatery, but not before Billy could yell, "Stop! Thief! Thief who isn't me!"

The Little People awoke with a start. Dumbledalf, who slept with his eyes, mouth, ears, and nose open, lay on the floor drooling. Buffer smacked him upside the head for a few

---

* It's like Yelp with a W . . . do I really have to keep explaining these?

minutes until he rose without so much as blinking, coughing, listening, or trimming his nose hairs.

"Someone has taken our ponies and disappeared behind the disappearing wall!"

"The poor unicorns!" exclaimed Dumbledalf. "Necromort probably drank them." Everybody would have asked who Necromort was if just then Billy hadn't spotted something less important.*

"I think this place is called Nino's Italian Eatery," speculated Billy, pointing at the sign that said "Nino's Italian Eatery." This was a legitimately good guess on the wobbit's part, considering his illiteracy.

"Moblins!" yelled Sorkinshield, just as six million Moblins began pouring out the reappearing front door. Some were in chef aprons, others in three-piece suits, but all had slicked-back hair and smelled of carnations and garlic. They rushed toward the YOLOers, snatching each one up until they reached Ballin and Drawlin.

"Are these guys with you?" they asked.

"We are mighty Little warriors," proclaimed Ballin and Drawlin.

"You don't look like the others. We thought all Little People looked identical." As proof, the Moblins pointed at Fili and Kiwi, who were struggling mightily in the massive arms of a fedora-wearing Moblin and pecking at a pile of seeds in the corner, respectively.

"But those two are very close-knit biological brothers!"

---

* In case you're wondering, reader, Necromort the Voldemancer is a deeply evil force in Widdle Wearth that Dumbledalf had mentioned many a time already on this quest. Nobody else has ever seen or heard of him.

protested Drawlin. This satisfied the Moblins, who dragged the two Little People away as they vigorously debated whether the moral victory of equal treatment they had just achieved was worth them and all of their friends getting killed by Moblins.

As they were shoved into the confectionary, one Moblin cackled. "Let's show our guests a good time . . . in Jersey."

The Little People shuddered in fear. Everyone with ears had heard stories of Old Jersey in the tales of old, and everyone without ears had smelled it as they were getting off the highway. There were scary places, and then there were deadly places, and then there was Jersey.

The inside of Holsten's looked like any ordinary diner, except that it went on forever and held thousands of booths and tables and bloodthirsty Moblins. The floor was covered in melted ice cream, bones of old enemies were stacked high in the corners, and framed pictures of Elf Pacino hung on the walls.

"Enjoy yourselves," the waiter implored, stopping to turn and shoot a Moblin stealing singles from the register. "The customers are family here."

"One order of the phoenix, please," said Dumbledalf, knocking over a couple of stools as he stumbled to the bar. He flipped a solid gold coin high into the air that landed in the bartender's shirt pocket. It was magical, although he had been aiming for the tip jar.

"Not in this inner-mountain confectionary," said the bartender, removing the coin and returning it to the wizard.

Dumbledalf shook his head sternly. This time he removed a coin from behind the bartender's ear. The wizard had been practicing for weeks, although he had planned on just removing the ear.

"Maybe you didn't hear him the first time," said a voice from the corner-most corner table. The Little People and Billy turned to face a stocky, balding Moblin with a gravelly voice and a gooey tuft of chest hair poking out from his bowling shirt.

They knew him at once. It was *the* Moblin, Tony Moblin, numero uno according to the official counting system of Old Jersey.* Tony Moblin had ordered the hits on Sorkinshield's family that had started the Moblin–Little People wars so many years ago.

"Well, well, well." He smiled in a bad way. "If it isn't Aaron Sorkinshield. I remember personally killing your father's father. If I recall, he was very mortal."

Sorkinshield took a quick glance around and sized up their chances. "How many henchmen you got? Eight, nine hundred?"

"Six million. All here and accounted for." Moblins were legendarily trustworthy accountants.

"I heard you've grown power hungry," said Beefer, taking the opportunity to carbo-load with a huge plate of pasta on which he'd poured a pile of Metamucil. "You sure you can trust all your men? Out of six million, there must be at least one rat."

Dumbledalf tapped his staff on the floor, turning Tony's consigliere into a giant rat. He had been trying for a piece of cake.

"Run, Hairy! You're a wizard!"

"You're the wizard," cried Billy.

"*I'm* the wizard," confirmed Dumbledalf, and began to

---

* Numero Uno, Papa John's, Domino's, five.

throw chairs at the Moblins, accidentally creating a diversion that gave the others a head start.

But Billy quickly remembered how hard it is to run fast when you are very, very slow. Just when he only had nine-tenths of the way to the exit left to go, a hand lurched out and grabbed the wobbit by the throat. He was reeled in and thrust atop a giant bowl of spumoni, face-to-face with Tony Moblin himself.

"You look a little big for a Little Person," Tony remarked, licking his spoon.

Billy, who was obviously not a Little Person, thought he might be able to fool Tony even still. "I'm one of you guys," he stammered. "My name is Wobbit De Niro."

"So you're a wise guy, huh?" Tony's theory was that most wise guys were wizards, a theory Dumbledalf did everything in his power to disprove.

Billy surveyed the diner, taking in the total chaos. Amidst the six million Moblins, nary a Little Person could be found. And then—crawling through the saturated legs of the Moblins, assembling ingredients for a tomato-mozzarella-eggplant protein shake as they went, came Beefer and Buffer!

Billy smiled at the dramatic irony. "Say hello to my little friends."

The onslaught of flying eggplants assaulted Tony before he could raise a hand. Billy seized his chance and bolted for the exit in the back of the restaurant, jogging the quickest he had ever jogged. His secret was being in mortal danger and forgetting to breathe.

He burst through the door and dove into a nearby trash Dumpster. He thought it wise to hide and chew on some two-day-old fettuccine until he was out of danger or got food poisoning, whichever came first. For thirty minutes he sat inside the Dumpster, reminded of the simpler days when he lived in a hole in the ground next to friendly wobbits and polite terrorists.

Just then the door swung open and he heard the pitter-patter of Little People feet dart through the exit with the pitta'-patta' of Moblin feet hot on their heels. As they chased his friends into the mountain of Old Jersey, they sang a terrifying song. Its words would strike fear into any heart, even if its melody would make those same hearts desperately want to fall in love.

> *Borgatà! Omertà!*
> *La Cosa Nostra!*
> *Head down to Jersey*
> *Like you're supposed ta!*

> *Goodfellas and goombahs!*
> *Bada boom! Bada bing!*
> *Like Marciano we fight*
> *And Sinatra we sing!*

> *Columbo! Luciano!*
> *Gambino! Capone!*
> *The factories we run*
> *And the unions we own!*

The singing continued for what seemed like ages, and that first line didn't even rhyme. The Moblins followed the Little People deep into the tunnels and forgot all about Billy, who was about as memorable as most of the Billys you know. When the coast was clear, he hopped out of the Dumpster, covered in Parmesan cheese. After a quick half hour of shedding most of his clothes and licking himself clean, he continued his trek into the depths of the mountain.

Several roads stretched out before Billy. Some were twisty and turny, others spiraled downward for miles, and two roads diverged in a yellow wood. The wobbit took the one less traveled by, but it didn't really make a difference because they ended up working stuff out and coming together again. The path grew darker and darker until Billy couldn't see where he was going. He would've been able to smell where he was going, if where he was going was the pot roast factory and his nose hadn't been plugged up with Parmesan. Far behind him he could hear the Moblins contemplating what to do.*

"I ain't going any farther. You know what's down there."

"They tried to whack the boss. We don't have a choice."

"I mean . . . we kind of have a choice."

"What do you mean?"

"You know how we're all butchers?"

"Sure."

"What if we started actually butchering?"

"Like, no more fronts? Just actual butcheries?"

"We retire from the game, play it straight. For our families. For our children's children. We stick to killing animals. What do you say?"

"What about the rats?"

"They're animals. So of course we still whack the rats."

Billy was thoroughly frightened by the Moblins' reluctance to go farther. He kept bumping into stalagmites, running into

---

* The Parmesan in his ears actually seemed to be helping.

stalactites, and falling headfirst down the occasional flight of stairs. Making little progress, he decided to take a rest and look for directions. Of course, his 3G service had no bars inside the mountain, and he was relegated to a few quick games of Tetris to calm his nerves. He pushed onward into the depths of Old Jersey, his phone's flashlight app leading the way.

Back in Holsten's Brookdale Confectionary, Tony Moblin was sucking down spumoni with anger. He had missed his chance to kill Sorkinshield, mortal enemy and rival screenwriter. The other Moblins knew better than to disturb him, plus most of them were trying to get the consigliere out of a mousetrap.

He decided to take solace in his family, inviting them to join him over a basket of onion rings. At the end of the day, even if there were no identifiable days inside of a mountain, what else really mattered in life?* Then the front door swung open, a bell rung, Tony looked up, and the chapter ended with a bang.

---

* The *Harvard Lampoon* leaves this question open for debate and discussion in your book circles and prison reading groups.

✡

The Plotz Thickens

N ow certainly Billy was in a tight place, or, as wobbits call it, indoors. The tunnel he had wandered into seemed to have no end, and he was beginning to think that holding his breath for good luck might not have been the best idea. He exhaled, which quickly turned into a yawn, which quickly turned into eating a sandwich, which slowly turned into the realization that a sandwich made out of rocks and bats was going to be just as much trouble coming out as it was going in. As is the tradition in long, noble quests to regain the rightful home of a lost people, it had been nearly five chapters since anybody in Billy's party had relieved themselves. Billy himself had been waiting for the right moment, but he'd gotten the distinct feeling that there was always somebody watching him who would share his every bowel movement with an embarrassingly middle-aged audience in a homey, lighthearted style.*

---

* *Widdle Wearth's Next Top Bowel Movement* is currently the second-most popular show in the land. The most popular is, of course, *Breaking Bad*.

It was in this state of looking for a handicap-accessible bathroom (he had not yet quite lowered himself to the humiliation of a regular stall), that he came upon a tiny ring of cold metal lying on the floor of a tunnel. It was a turning point in his career though he did not know it, as he couldn't decipher the invitation to LinkedIn that Necromort the Voldemancer had carved on the inside. It did, however, fill his head with unpleasant little whispers about the corrupting influence of power and how potency (or perhaps potentiality), if it is to be exercised and produce results, has to be externalized and so passes, to a greater or lesser degree, out of one's direct control. All told, it was a fairly tiresome, self-important piece of jewelry, and Billy quickly tossed it aside when he came upon an even shinier anklet a few yards away.

On and on he went, and down and down, and still he heard no sound of anything except the occasional thought that going on and on and down and down was a very bad way to stop being underground. He briefly considered taking the 405, which would have been suicide at this time of day, and even more briefly considered taking the bus, which would have been homicide at pretty much any time of its eternal night. I do not know how long he kept on like this, hating to go on, not daring to stop, and completely unaware of the fact that steady-rate cardio is a prohibitively inefficient way of burning calories while building muscle. If I had to guess, though: probably about ten or fifteen minutes.

Suddenly, and without any warning besides the increasing dampness of the air and the changing consistency of the ground and a bunch of kitschy surf shops, Billy trotted—*splash!*—into water. He tested it and tasted it to make sure, hoping against hoping that he may have stumbled on the fabled Biggest Gulp. But there was no trace of corn syrup in the vile concoction. This did remind Billy, however, that he still had a little regular syrup left in his flask, so he promptly sat down to rehydrate and pass out for a half hour of dreamless shame-sleep.

Deep down there by the other side of the water lived old Goldstein, a small, unathletic creature. I don't know where he came from, nor who or what he was. He was Goldstein, as fair skinned as SPF 30 and a sensible hat on a hot day in the park would allow. Truly he was a frightening apparition, though this was mainly due to his hair, which simply had a mind of its own in moisture like this, and when he was out there all day on the boat, oy *vey,* forget it, he would just shave it off, but his *bubbe* would never forgive him, and anyway she's been through enough, hasn't she, bless her heart. He loved company but rarely got it, as the Moblins sensed that the depths of the cave just weren't their kind of neighborhood, and even the fish would rather he find his own slimy pool of darkness to swim in. So when Goldstein saw Billy stirring from his sugar nap, he got up from his strange feast and called out to him.

"Hey there! You! The schlemiel who looks like he ate the schlimazel! You look like a man who wouldn't miss the chance to put a little more nosh in that *tuchus.*"

And when Goldstein said that last word, he made a horrible swallowing noise in his throat, the likes of which Billy had never heard anywhere in Widdle Wearth. Billy nearly jumped out of his skin, which is precisely why wobbits do their best to always have a lot of extra skin.

"Wh-wh-what are you?" Billy stammered.

"What am I? Well, if you ask my mother, I'm a trial sent straight from God to test her tender heart! I'll tell you what, though, that was a woman. Kvetch and kvetch all you want, but she'd never hear a word of it, and bless her heart if it didn't take a lot of chutzpah to raise this little terror. She always said she'd throw me right into Mordor one day and I wouldn't put it past her to do it. After all, one does not simply walk into temple without first saying hello to Grandpa George and Rabbi—*oy!*"

Goldstein had a habit of talking to himself, which Billy found so unnerving that he had come across the lake just to stab the fiend in the side with his sword.

"Shalom to you too, little pharaoh." Goldstein winced, bandaging his wound with self-deprecating humor and the help of the first aid kit he always had handy. "Your people call that a conversion, mine call it a Tuesday. Still, this is a seder, not a bris, so how about you trade in the dagger for a piece of matzo and a cup of wine."

"I am Mr. Billy Bagboy," Billy squealed. "I have lost the Little People and I have lost the wizard and I don't know where I am and I don't want to know, if only I can get away."

"Feh! Get away! I tried that once. I figured why waste the miles, get down to Florida, convince my dad that the crocodiles weren't stealing from him and the egrets weren't speaking German. I fly United; what do I know? I'm telling you, you're better off taking a stagecoach than flying coach, and this is coming from a guy who only needs one leg's worth of leg room between the two of them—*ow!*"

"This is a sword, a blade that was forged to kill Moblins."

"Baby, a lifetime of sausage and simple carbs will take care of that for you. Now *ha lachma anya* and yada yada and all that, come, have a seat. Elijah won't mind; he never shows up anyway. I'm assuming you don't know the four questions?"

Billy had heard of these deadly sorts of riddle games, played by only the most evil, diabolical creatures, or anybody on day two or three of a road trip.

"Very well, creature," said Billy, summoning his courage. "I'll play your game. If you win, you may eat me. But if I win, you must show me the way out of here."

Goldstein laughed this off, prone to mistaking funny ideas for humor. "All right," he said. "Me first. Now: *Why is this night different from all other nights?*"

Billy had never heard this riddle before, and he attempted to think deeply about it. He went about as deep as his stomach before the answer came grumbling out of him:

"I'm hungry!"

"That's about as good an answer as I ever got. They don't call matzo the bread of affliction for nothing."

"Ha! Now it's my turn, beast!"

"Well, okay, a little unorthodox to take turns, but once you start the Reform, who am I to stop it? Go ahead, win one more for the goyim."

Billy knew his life depended on this riddle, so he tried to think of something complex, whose every intellectual twist and turn would leave Goldstein gasping for air and begging for mercy. Something that seemed simple and elegant but held the key to a vast and ancient wisdom. All of which seemed fairly difficult, so Billy just said a bunch of stupid things in a row:

It cannot be seen, cannot be felt,
Cannot be heard, cannot be smelt.
It lies behind stars and under hills,

And empty holes it fills.
It comes first and follows after,
Ends life, kills laughter.

Billy was rather proud of this one, and thought he must
have read it on his cousin's Tumblr at one point or another. But
Goldstein barely hesitated:

"The housing bubble! That's an easy one! Optimus Prime,
overwritten. It's all bubkes anyway, but try telling that to my
brother Jerry before he starts bundling Ents and saying tree
houses are never going to stop going up. We'll see what kills
his laughter in a month or two, that's all I'm saying. Pop one
bubble and there's another swelling up faster than my great-
aunt's goiter."

As usual, Billy had no idea what Goldstein was talking
about, so he responded by stabbing him in the leg again.

"*Baruch atah* and my thigh, that hurts! Don't you know
the classics, at least? If you prick us, do we not bleed? If you
stab us repeatedly, does it not aggravate our stress-induced
asthma?"

This was the hardest riddle yet for Billy, as it seemed both
satirical and rhetorical, two words that he had no time to look
up. Plus, stabbing Goldstein seemed to work just about as well
as trying to understand him, and somehow it seemed to fit in
better with the grand sweep of history.

"Ow! Ow! Ow! All right already, all right! In my day we
had to call up at least four or five of the plagues to get out of a
seder, but the Macabees just ain't what they used to bees. I can
show you the way out. Just let me get a napkin and I'll write
it down for you. The street signs are *shmutz* down here. I've
been trying to get the city council to fix them for months, but

they're all in somebody's pocket or else they're just half in the bag, and I'm not saying I'm a picture of perfect health but if I was more shiksa and less schmuck, maybe then . . ."

As Goldstein trailed off into a soothing rhythm of complaint, Billy started searching his pockets for food. What he found instead was the anklet he had picked up before. He had always wondered if he could pull off an anklet, but the necessary combination of flexibility and having a locatable ankle had always stopped him. This anklet, however, slipped on perfectly, which, in Billy's mind, meant he managed to squeeze it between two equidistant, shapeless fat rolls without causing a chain reaction.

Suddenly he felt the heady rush of high fashion and lowered circulation. Meanwhile, Goldstein had finally found both a napkin and a working pen in the very back of one of his many drawers.

"Here we are! So you're just going to take the first left out of here, and then . . . Billy?"

Goldstein looked around in bewilderment, and Billy thought it must be because of his new and daring accessory. He hopped away from the table and began to gloat, which he normally reserved for hot-dog eating contests and buttered-cat swallowing tournaments.

"That's right, you filthy trickster! I've won your game and I've stolen your anklet! And no matter how much you obsess over it and covet it, I'll never give it back!"

"You found my anklet? I was wondering what became of it. Well, see now, I'd really prefer it if you didn't take it. It belonged to my grandmother, and it's really all I have left of her after—okay! Again with the stabbing! In the spirit of Passover, I give it to you. Mazel tov."

"Aha! I've tricked you again! And now I'm taking it and I'm leaving!"

"Okay, but make sure to keep it out of water, and you might get it polished every so often. I know a guy who does that sort of thing, and he's *prettay, prettayyyy, prettayyyyyy—*"

But before Goldstein could even finish his catchphrase, Billy stabbed him again, pelted him with a few rocks, and took off into the dark mountain, leaving Goldstein to wish he had followed his mother's advice and become a doctor all those years ago.

VI

Treehuggers and Muddafuggers

It goes without saying that somewhere between chapters five and six, Billy found his way out of the mountain. But the backside of a mountain is no place to know where you are. He was terribly lost and had already had quite enough of this YOLO.

His apparel had fared little better. He had lost his hood, cloak, belt, trousers, and shoes, and he was now almost completely naked save his fashion-forward anklet.

He waddled down a stony path and sat down firmly on a rock stump to think about where to go and what to do. He looked forward, then backward, then forward again until he was out of breath and deliriously fantasizing about his wobbit-hole, which he was beginning to think of as his own little anti-mountain.

He knew he had a decision to make. Now that he had in his possession an anklet that complimented his figure, his self-confidence was at an all-time high. But with good looks came great responsibility, and, based on the episodic nature of this quest, Billy knew that his friends were probably in grave danger right about now. A hero in the same circumstances might consider it his duty to go back and save his friends, murdering any bit characters and extras that got in his way. But was our poor wobbit a hero? He rose valiantly in the shining light of the afternoon, his anklet glistening with courage sweat. Only he could single-handedly defeat the six million Moblins, revive the half of his friends that were certainly already dead, and carry everyone to safety out of a complex labyrinthine mountain that he had no idea how to navigate.

"Whom am I kidding," he said intelligently. He sat back down and tried eating a slug he'd found on the ground. It was a wise decision, for not a moment after he'd given up on his ragtag crew of Little People did he hear voices in the fields below. He crept around a convenient rock that was just about wobbit-tall and just a little less than wobbit-wide.

"I miss the bagboy," he heard Whorey whine. "He made me feel so not-fat. Pretending that he's that rock over there that's shaped exactly like him is totally not making me feel better about myself." She sighed. Slorey and Kourtney looked at her in confusion. "Because it's a rock, and a rock's not a living thing," she clarified, and Slorey and Kourtney nodded with their normal amount of confusion.

Hearing this delighted our clogged wobbit's heart. He wheeled around and looked on the other side of the rock.

There before him was Ballin, standing guard (and not, it is worth mentioning, because everybody else presumed he would look the most intimidating to enemies. They just believed he was the most capable to carry out the task due to his years of experience at standing guard, which he had gotten because people always presumed him to be the most intimidating).

"I will give him a surprise," Billy thought, and threw a handful of confetti in his face. Yet Ballin did not react other than to wipe some dirt off his shoulder. Unfazed, Billy waited patiently to be appreciated.

He began to notice something curious. Though Ballin was standing right in front of Billy, he was looking everywhere *except* right at the wobbit. When Billy moved to one side and wobbled his hands about, Ballin reflexively looked the other direction. When Billy headed for *that* direction, Ballin would again promptly look away. This continued for some time until Billy's arms wobbled themselves to exhaustion and Ballin was stricken with an inexplicable headache.

Billy proceeded past Ballin nervously, beginning to doubt how attractive his anklet truly was.

He stationed himself in the center of the camp. The Little People and Dumbledalf carried on as if he wasn't there.

"We can't leave him behind. After all, he is my friend," said the wizard. "I have a friend. At least one friend." He thoughtfully yanked out whole tufts of his beard. His voice lowered solemnly. "Although I think he might be half a blood."*

"All this talking without walking is giving me a terrible migraine," said Sorkinshield. The others nodded, feeling flashes of pain in their prefrontal cortexes as well. It was as though they had paid four or five extra dollars to experience something that was definitely worse than the original experience.

"It's like all I can see is a distorted reality playing out before my eyes," continued Sorkinshield, who was really, really high.

Billy did not appreciate being spoken of as though he was

---

* Like most wobbits, Billy was actually more of a muddy-blood, meaning his blood was half blood and half milk chocolate.

not present. He was about to get angry, but instead took three deep breaths, counted to ten, and realized the real issue. The Little People and the wizard were far too sensible to associate themselves with anyone wearing an anklet so brazenly.

"Fine, fine," Billy acquiesced. "I understand. I'll remove the anklet." He shoved a few fat rings out of the way and wrenched the thing off.

"Welcome back!" his friends shouted with delight as soon as his anklet's clasp was released. "Hooray!" they cheered, the proper manner of speaking in unison for such a YOLO occasion.

When spirits returned to their usual depressingly low level, Ballin approached the wobbit.

"How ever did you get by me?" he asked, quite impressed. "Normally I'm a highly skilled guard. Due to my experience."

"What we have here is perhaps a case of reverse racism," Billy speculated. "Can I not be an equally skilled burglar due to my *lack* of experience?"

None of them followed his lack of logic, but they figured if they relieved him of his nakedness, maybe he'd stop saying uncomfortable things about race. So Ballin lent Billy the hood of his cloak to cover himself, and Loin assisted in fashioning it into a cloth. Then they wanted to know all about his adventures after they had lost him, and he told them everything at once, stopping only four times for wheezing and three times for some cake.

"What did I tell you?" laughed Dumbledalf. "Hairy has more about him than you guess." He gave Billy a queer look, his eyes half-twinkling, half-drugged.

Then Billy had questions of his own to ask, for he wished to know how his friends had escaped the grasp of the Moblins.

"A rather ticklish business," Loin said. "Touch and go! But Dumbledalf knew about the back door, and once you know about it, it's just a matter of getting through it. It was a wooden door, so we used axes." Everyone groaned in disappointment, especially since Loin could've made *something* out of wood.

"I know my way around the dark," explained Dumbledalf. "I'm not a wizard for nothing. I am a wizard." He paused. Everyone waited eagerly for the rest of what he had to say, but he only stared at the grass and hummed a John Williams theme to himself.*

Just then a battle cry echoed down from the mountains.

"It seems as though the Moblins are on to us," said somebody. Honestly, I can't remember who. Probably Drawlin or something. Whatever.

Sorkinshield took the opportunity to make a short speech about courage in the face of six million equally courageous mountain creatures. Then they all gathered in a huddle and high-fived one another before setting off as fast as they could. The Moblins were in non-trivial pursuit, riding atop an army of wargis. Though Billy had never seen one before, the breed had a reputation for being fiercely adorable.†

All of a sudden a clearing opened up before the party. They stopped at once, awestruck. Beneath the full moon, scrunched on tiny hind legs, sat the cutest little wargi pup they'd ever

---

* If you purchased one of the *Lampoon*'s Speak-O-Books, scratch here until you hear the theme:

† Ah, wargis. They look much like you'd expect. Comically huge and heavy head atop a fur-ball body barely held up by puffs of legs. Imagine a puppy from our generation that was run through a cute machine and then given the love and attention of a brutal, broken Moblin whose life has otherwise been reduced to a constant fear of death and stereotype fulfillment. Now imagine feeding that wargi peanut butter.

seen, adorably licking its genitals. The wargi rolled over and pawed the ground, but its futile attempts at ferocity only made it cuter. Kourtney could not help herself, and I suspect you would not have done much better. She ran forward, sweeping the wargi off the ground and tossing the furry fiend into her purse.

"A poochie in a Gucci," she whispered, tearing up.

It was a trap, of course. No sooner did the wargi begin to vomit in Kourtney's purse than six million Moblins surrounded them from all sides.

A Moblin henchman strutted forth and wiped the remnants of a cannoli from his stubble. "Looks like you're outnumbered, fourteen to six million. To win this fight you'd either need an army of over five million or exactly three hundred."

Billy and the others looked around, surveying their options. They had somehow crossed into a vacant landscape with nowhere to run.* Surrounding them was nothing but a nuclear bunker, an armory, a time machine, and a tree.

With no other choice, they scurried up the tree.

You would have laughed (from an omniscient perspective) if you had seen the Little People there, sitting high up in the branches of the tree like they were giants with little heads and trees for bodies. Their beards swung beneath them, dangling perilously close to the ground. Billy had always been afraid of heights; it is no secret he only felt safe below ground level. Even when standing *at* ground level, the view down was terrifying. He could free-fall four and a half feet to his death at any moment.

---

* Trust me, dear reader; the topography of Widdle Wearth is complex and multi-faceted. Didn't you see that impressive map?

So staring down from the soaring heights of the larch tree was enough to make Billy lose his appetite, and not just because larch was difficult to chew and was mildly choking Billy at present.

He continued eating the larch leaves anyway, confident that somebody else was coming up with a grand escape plan. Kiwi puffed out his plumage and widened his eyes, the natural response of the Southern Brown Kiwi to a predator or other threat, while Fili looked at things, which is the natural response to any situation of a character whose only real trait is that he can see well. Meanwhile, Dumbledalf was too busy hanging upside down and saying "Whee!" to help much with an escape, and Sorkinshield was already furiously writing a note to his agent about getting a new quest on basic cable.

There was, however, one very convenient piece of good news, and it was this: neither Moblins nor wargis could climb a tree. Run an integrated mob syndicate? Sure. Sing their hearts out to a catchy, spontaneously composed tune? Who can't? But climb a tree? Not a chance.

With this in mind, Sorkinshield proposed the only sensible plan: "We'll just wait it out." He'd seen this work a thousand times in the movies he'd written.

As though on cue, the Moblins broke out into song. Sorkinshield had read the situation perfectly.*

Bunch of Little People sitting in a tree
K-i-s-s-i-n-g
First comes love

---

* To you budding writers who would like to craft a completely true story as grand as mine one day, I offer this advice: learn to read.

Then comes marriage
Then comes baby in a baby carriage!
Then comes school,
Then comes mortgage,
Then comes disappointment, divorce, alimony, emotional scarring,
  a second mortgage, remarriage, another baby in a nicer
  baby carriage, which makes the first baby kind of jealous
  but it's time for him to grow up, get his act together, and
  meet a nice girl so he can start this whole thing over again.

Sorkinshield hated song and frivolity in general. He blamed the whole mess on Kourtney and her wargi obsession.

"You just did a big thing badly. Get out of my office!" he shouted at the three sisters, gesturing toward a branch on which he'd written "Aaron Sorkinshield: Currently for Hire!"

"We just wanted to have fun!" set up Whorey.

"We're just girls!" continued Slorey.

"Girls just want to have fun!" Kourtney concluded, properly executing for the first time in her life the transitive property of equality.

But the fact remained that the Little People needed to do something to calm the hubbub transpiring below them. It was not a good sign that the Moblins were patient enough to write another verse and rehearse the lyrics to perform together in a six-million-part chorus.

Daaaaa dada daaaa da Da Da
Thaaaat is the theme to The Godfather
Just so it's clear what we're referencing
It's The Godfather.

Sorkinshield couldn't stand that somebody was singing when he hadn't written it into the screenplay. He was coming to his wits' end. There was nothing he could do. Everything was black. Then he opened his eyes, and everything was normal-colored again but still bad.

"You know, the word 'patriot' means a lot of things," he said. "It's about seeing things through, about loving what matters, about acing every test you've ever been given using the only tool out there: the truth. Here's the truth: 'repatriate' is a word that sounds a lot like 'patriot.' It means to take back. I think it's high time we take all we have left, boys: our lives."

Of course they'd all heard him say that a hundred times before. Nobody believed he would actually take his life and jump from the tree. A man of his eloquence could not simply fall. He had to be felled.

But they were wrong. It was a plot twist they should have seen coming from a man like Sorkinshield. He let go of the wind-slapped boughs to an audience full of gasps, tumbling down through both the pines *and* the cones toward a 100 percent certain death, plus or minus a 10 percent margin of error.

And yet—someone must have rounded up the statistics! Just as Sorkinshield's biopic's trailer was flashing before his eyes, he was snatched out of the air by the red-hot hands of six-time Pro Bowler and star receiver for the 2004 Philadelphia Eagles, Terrell Owens.

"Touchdown!" Owens declared, dancing in the chaos and spiking Sorkinshield into the ground. Before anyone could comprehend what was going on, Eagles running back Brian Westbrook swept Fili, Kiwi, Slorey, Whorey, and Kourtney into his bosom and charged down the field. Beefer and Buffer found refuge in 2004 NFC Offensive Player of the Year Donovan McNabb's embrace, and were one by one tossed in perfect spirals to wide receiver Greg Lewis. Linebacker Jeremiah Trotter scooped up the rest, and Billy and Dumbledalf rode his shoulder pads. This was a bit lopsided due to Billy's great weight and Dumbledalf's lack of bone density, but nothing could stop the Eagles when victory was on the line.

Billy could not believe their luck. The 2004 NFC Champion Philadelphia Eagles were the most majestic creatures in the land. While lesser species flew, the Eagles soared straight to a 27–10 victory over the Atlanta Falcons in the NFC Championship.

The all-star roster deposited Billy and his friends in the safety of the Eagles' locker room, where they sprayed one another with champagne from bottle after bottle, slapped buttock after buttock, and generally provided Loin and Groin with a host of material that the two chose to respectfully pass on.

After the obligatory revelry had been had, a hush fell over the locker room, and Eagles head coach Andy Reid entered stoically. He was as gallant as the legends claimed, and more adorable than a wargi. One day he might rise up to be the king of all the birds, which is an actual monarchy that for complicated sociopolitical reasons all birds are okay with.

"I heard you were stuck up a tree, as they say," said the brave leader of the Eagles. "I owed Dumbledalf a favor from a few years back—he drew up quite the trick play for us in the 2004 NFC Championship game against those good-for-nothing Falcons. Not even I knew where the ball was, and it hasn't been spotted since."

Dumbledalf blushed and removed the football from beneath his cloak.

Coach Reid cawed pleasantly and took the ball in his conference-winning hands. "Perhaps it's time for some light-hearted fun then. Anyone up for a scrimmage?"

Needless to say, everyone was up for a scrimmage. The Little People lined up against their saviors.

The Philadelphia Eagles won.

VII

Dänsing in the Dårk

The next morning Billy awoke to the soft stab of morning sun and a breakfast of cold mutton he must have tucked underneath one of his teats long ago. He was groggily wiping his mouth when a broad-shouldered figure slapped what wound up being his inner thigh.

"Ready to roll, Billy?" Wide receiver Greg Lewis!

Billy hopped on Lewis's back with a sigh. "Ready as I'll ever be, Ocho-Tres."

The great creature whooped and sprinted to catch up with his teammates. Wind whistled past the wobbit's caulifloral ears as he nestled down among Lewis's abundant triceps.

The team made for the hills, sprinting and leapfrogging one another, and occasionally retrieving Doc, who kept falling headfirst off his Eagle, painfully reminding everyone of the dangers of chronic head trauma in football as well as the fact that Doc existed. But then it was time to put the fun aside and return to YOLO-as-usual. The Eagles wished them a strong season and headed back to their locker room, where ice baths, hot towels, and lukewarm cheerleaders awaited.

"May the wind under your wings bear you where the sun sails and the moon walks!" exclaimed Dumbledalf, though it was unclear to whom he was exclaiming. "Catch the queefle!" he added, making it all too clear that he was just exclaiming for the fun of it.

The band marched onward. They crossed a stream and a rock and then another stream, which turned out to be, technically, the same stream. Exhausted, they stopped at the next same rock to regroup. Dumbledalf cleared his throat.

"It appears it's way-parting time," he began heavily. "You must act as you see fit, and I—I shall act."

At this he snapped on two white gloves, smeared black mud on his face, and began to sing the opening bars of "Toot, Toot, Tootsie! Goodbye!"

Ballin and Drawlin quickly put a stop to this new career.

"Very well. Still, I didn't anticipate coming even this far with you. This is, after all, Hairy's adventure." He turned his twinkling, disturbingly exaggerated eyes on the wobbit. "All I wanted was to see you through puberty. Now that I know how short and weird looking you wind up, it is time I take care of other business."

The Little People halfheartedly begged him to stay, though inwardly they were all a bit relieved to have a break from the old man, who had recently taken to referring to them as "Dumbledalf's Armoire" and stuffing his extra hats in their mouths.

". . . but first I will stay with you for a couple more chapters, because I have completely forgotten what that other business was," the wizard continued. He sensed it involved elves and was incredibly important and interesting, so important and interesting, in fact, that someone producing a bloated movie adaptation of their quest could just make it up later. "Oh well, breakfast time!"

Despite it being well into evening, Dumbledalf went on to outline their options in this land: a Denny's, a nice Greek diner, an IHOP, or Björn's house. Once the Little People realized he had stopped talking, they burst into debate, discussion, and a little bribery, none of which I will detail here.[*] They finally decided to go to Björn's house, because the bathroom would probably be cleaner there, and they all *really* needed to go by now. Besides, IHOP in Widdle Wearth stood for International House of Putridity, and Denny was more of a sci-fi guy.

Dumbledalf soon slowed to a walk alongside the wobbit. "I care about you very much, Hairy. Which is why I will tell you in advance of our destination, *do not stroll the corridors at night*. Also, *look what happens when I have important things to say*."

Billy found this to be sound advice. Wobbits have trouble both with strolling and with corridors, since they fall over doing the former and can't eat any part of the latter.

The sun was doing its final spiral down the great drain of the sky when Doc shrieked. Everybody assumed he was just having another one of his day terrors until they noticed a swarm of suspiciously hairy bumblebees in a clump of suspiciously antlered plants.

"If one of those things were to prick me, I'd swell to twice

---

[*] For greater descriptions of this and other deleted scenes, see *The Harvard Lampoon's The Similar-illian,* a book still seeking a publisher.

my size," moaned Loin. The others held out for something promisingly raunchy, but gave up upon remembering that Loin had very serious and life-threatening allergies.

A pregnant pause followed, which Dumbledalf soon aborted: "We have reached the driveway to Björn's house. You secondary characters should wait while Hairy and I go on ahead."

A line of horses approached them in the driveway. Like the bees and plants, however, there was something strange about these horses, like the fact that they were all seven feet tall and wore comically large top hats. Still, each one of them was clearly labeled "Normal Horsey Horse," and horse-labelers had never lied to Billy before, so he put aside his doubts and prepared himself to meet the man of the house. It was then that he realized the man of the house was already standing in front of him, though he was so dark and brooding that Billy had mistaken him for a mere shadow of the house.

"You are excused," Björn grunted to his beasts. "Go and do some normal horse things." Billy silently marveled at the intriguing enigma of the man before him. He had jet-black hair, so black that it almost seemed unnatural. His skin was a deep, oranged tan and, even though he stooped, he seemed as though he must be nearly twice as tall as the safe and reliable car parked outside his house.

Björn turned to Billy, sensing the wobbit's growing depression. "Who are you and what do you want?"

"I am Dumbledalf," said the smiling wizard. "And this is *Hairy*." He raised his eyebrows significantly at the giant man.

Björn adjusted his definitely real hair.

"*Hairy*," repeated Dumbledalf.

Björn cast his unremarkable, dark brown gaze over the rest

of the Little People, who had, of course, completely ignored Dumbledalf's command.

"I only harbor refugees from Moblins," Björn grunted. Everyone became rather dejected at hearing this until Drawlin explained what "refugee" meant.

Dumbledalf acquainted Björn with the true purpose of their quest while the others entered Björn's estate. Their host followed them in. With a clap of his great hands, fluorescent lights turned on and several massive dogs appeared from the adjoining massive-dog storage room.

"Bork bork bork!" said the dogs.

"Bark bark bark!" corrected Björn, as he adjusted their dog costumes and hurried them out of the room.

The not-dogs soon returned with great dishes of meatballs and berry parfaits on their strong backs. The weary travelers then had such a feast as they had not enjoyed since L. Ron's hospitality in Livinwell. As they ate, Björn swilled vodka from a secret flask and gave them advice for surviving the impending dark forest of Jerkwood and its enchanted river.* The Little People ignored what he said, having grown too frustrated by this point with their futile attempts to assemble their chairs.

It is a queer feature of Björn's part of the woods that the sun sets only briefly in summer months. It has something to do with how the sky works, and after that it is a total mystery. Thus, Billy had a hard time sleeping that night. He tried counting sheep, but there weren't more than a half dozen outside. He tried counting calories, but he loved each of them too dearly to objectify them like that. He tried to let the deep and very normal rhythm of the woods lull him to sleep, but he

---

* "Go around the impending dark forest of Jerkwood and its enchanted river."

slowly realized that ear-shattering, thumping bass isn't actually all that easy to sleep to. Then he remembered Dumbledalf's warning. What *did* happen in these woods at night?

"Oh, Billy, you really do have some Gram fat globules in there among the Bagboy," he thought to himself as he crept curiously to the window. He wiped the fog off the glass and watched for the mere seconds he had before his gaping mouth would fog the window back up again.

And what was that beat in the woods but the pounding of House music! And there in the very center of the multicolored light-up dance floor, among the fog machines and strobe lights, leading the revelry—their host! Björn would have been nearly unrecognizable if his original disguise had not been so transparent and terrible. He bobbed to the music with Nordic efficiency, his sculpted body raised to its full height and his beautiful blond hair let free from its mousy prison. His eyes were bluer than blue, and so bright that they seemed to light up the entire forest. Yes, Björn was a skin-changer, able to wash off the layers of bronzer he normally caked on to reveal the pale, luminescent flesh below. Nor did he revel alone: all the bumblebees and horses and plants and dogs had shed their sunglasses and trench coats, and Billy could now see them for what they were. They were moose, great and noble beasts that had converged on this spot to shake a well-subsidized and high-standard-of-living leg along with their Swedish master.

The next morning a visibly hungover Björn saddled up his most convincing ponies and sent their group off with provisions and good wishes. Billy remained quiet about what he saw, even when the Little People speculated about the glitter covering Björn's entire body.

"I too will leave you here," said Dumbledalf then, much to

their elated protestation. "Good-bye! Remember to never be centaurs." And off he wandered.

The rest rode north in somber silence to the fringe of great Jerkwood. As they marched single file into the gloom of the woods, it grew to be pitch-black. Not the pitch-blackness you and I have experienced in our comfortable bourgeois lives, but rather a fantasy-novel sort of pitch-blackness. The Little People could barely discern the path by day. At night they ate their meager rations around a lantern fueled by extra bacon grease Billy had found between his bacon.

Worse still, the darkness only amplified the voice of the forest. Quietly but aggressively, it blew through the branches of the trees and just acted like a total jerk.

"Look at this, a kindergarten field trip," it said smugly the first night. "Is that a beard, or just a hairy bib your mommy makes you wear?" Hearing this, Buffer punched wildly at the darkness, but the voice of Jerkwood only chuckled.

"Perhaps you will prevail in this journey after all," it commented one night at dinner, as Billy prepared to bite into his meager supper. "But you will never stop being four feet tall."

Indeed, all the wildlife in that morbid place bore marks of Jerkwood's bullying. The adventurers' daily slog took them past drooping flowers and moss-covered rocks gone prematurely bald.

One day, at last, they reached a roaring current. A river! And a boat on the other shore! What a jerk this forest was.

Billy and the Little People set to scheming. No one could recall Björn's warnings about the water's enchantments, but they remembered it had the effect of dampening clothes. Determined thus to reel in the boat, they tied a hook to a rope

and told Beefer to throw it into the vessel. Beefer nodded
feebly, as the forest had brought out all the insecurities he had
spent his entire life overcompensating for.

He gave it a hurl and missed.

"Nice shot," came the smug voice of Jerkwood. "Do you
even lift?"

Incensed, Beefer decided to go heavy or go home, and his
inability to do the latter was kind of the whole point of this
quest. He tied the rope around Doc and hoisted him above his
head. He then spun around several times and flung his unnecessary friend out across the water, thus simultaneously inventing the sport of midget tossing and the art of involuntary scuba
diving. This time the rope clattered promisingly into the boat,
and Doc fell with a slightly more worrying clatter amongst the
sharp rocks on the other side. "Complete success!" hollered
Beefer. Billy and several Little People joined him on the rope
and hauled as Whorey, Slorey, and Kourtney did nothing and
Sorkinshield did nothing importantly.

The boat didn't move! It must have been tethered to the
other bank, which is literally the only reason a rowboat would
be staying in one place in the middle of a large flowing river.

"No pulling-out method will ever work!" ejaculated Groin
despairingly. "I can go into the physics if you'd like."*

The Little People are a feisty and persistent people, however, with a fairly serious Napoleon complex (and an even
more serious Oedipus complex, which explains why it was
so important to them to force their way back into the dark,
enclosed cavern where they were born). At last they brought

---

* $v^2 = v_0{}^2 + 2a\,(x - x_0)$.

the boat to shore and crossed. But just as the last of them were reaching the other side, Buffer noticed the prone figure of Doc, and in reaching to hoist him out, lost the boat.

"No turning back now," remarked Billy. Until then it had always been a legitimate possibility.

The others were trying in vain to awaken the still bleeding Doc. They concluded that the jagged rocks he had hit his head on must have been enchanted with some sort of strange sleeping spell.

"He looks cute when he sleeps," observed Slorey. "Look at him spasm! It's like he's dancing in his dreams." They all agreed that it was adorable and decided to wipe the foam from his mouth and keep going.

Suddenly Fili stopped dead along the path. "Say, is that a bluesy concert poster pegged to that tree?" They squinted at the red oak.

"*You're* a bluesy concert poster," spat back Jerkwood, then coughed quietly. Heckling could be a difficult business, even for a forest. Disregarding the crickets chirping in the background, they all agreed it was a concert poster.

With music dancing in their minds and filling their hearts and bloating their souls, they soon became convinced they could hear just such a concert in the distance. They would run toward it, glimpsing a lithe figure in a shining cape performing for an arena of jiving fans—only for the scene to vanish before their eyes. The letdown of these hallucinations was horrible, especially for Doc, who was still unconscious.

What eventually awoke Doc, of all things, was an old wobbit song sung by Billy. It just so happens that most wobbit songs are orchestrated for one voice and one sword hit against a big rock. Really, they are just a sequence of swallowing noises over arrhythmic clanging sounds, but they were loud and discordant enough to wake up Doc with a start.

"You and I just saved a Little Person through the power of music alone!" gasped Billy proudly to his little blade before sheathing it. "I must call you *Sting*."

His heroism had barely sunk in before a huge spider dropped into their midst. I mean, seriously, this thing was massive. Sorkinshield, Fili, Kiwi, Beefer, Buffer, Loin, and Groin blanched. Whorey, Kourtney, and Slorey blanched to the roots of their tans, which wasn't far. Drawlin and Ballin blanched just like anybody else would, because why wouldn't they? Doc, having just awoken, was not allowed to blanch for three weeks.

Billy blanched hardest, for this was, like, pretty much the biggest spider he had ever seen. At least an inch and a half across, legs akimbo, it treaded softly toward them with death in its eyes and at least enough poison in its fangs to make you itch for a week or so. Not even a small dead leaf in its path could slow down this monstrosity for more than a minute, and as it drew closer, the Little People held an urgent council to decide who should face it down.

"Beefer! Buffer!" clamored Loin and Groin.

"How about you pipsqueaks instead?" snarled Buffer, who had always felt intimidated by creatures who could perform more simultaneous arm curls than him.

"Me? I would have no clue where to stick it! And I have no protection!" cried Loin defensively.

"Seriously, do you not hear that setup?" shot back Beefer. "You have one job on this journey!"

Whorey smiled, feeling at home in petty debate.

"Maybe we should send Fili in there, since Kiwi can carry

on their mutual genes even in the event of his death," suggested Slorey practically.

"We are *not* brothers," sputtered Fili.

"Don't forget me, losers!" interjected the voice of Jerkwood.

"Sadly, they don't realize they are two hundred paces from the forest's edge," thought yours truly.

Just then Kourtney shrieked. The spider had crawled up her ankle. She passed immediately into a dead faint. Refusing to be outdone, Whorey and Slorey released a fragrance called Dead Faint and then passed out as well.

Beefer, Buffer, Loin, and Groin too lay on the ground, having knocked each other senseless. Sorkinshield and Drawlin were busy restraining a still-sputtering Fili, and the spider seized this opportunity to weave a web between Sorkinshield's and Drawlin's shoulders. Billy and Ballin rushed to their rescue but got another spiderweb all over their faces, giving them a deathly scare. Meanwhile, confused by all the hubbub, Kiwi decided to calm his nerves by eating the spider.

Before anyone could appreciate this anticlimax, into the clearing burst a colorful gang.* They gathered up the prostrate figures of Billy and the Little People and bound them in rope. Kiwi cocked his head curiously, which they thought was cute so they took him too.

Had they been in any state, our adventurers would have recognized their captors as figures from their strange earlier visions; but they were not in any state. They were in a forest, and soon they would be in a kingdom.

---

* Do not fear, dear reader. I know exactly how to structure a story. Every word here is written with the knowledge that I will one day expand this children's bedtime tale into two thousand pages of complex adult literature.

VIII

Rockabilly Bagboy

The trees had been tampered with in these parts, condemned to a fate worse than deforestation. By the light of elven torches, the captured YOLOers could see that indeed an endless supply of concert posters were tacked upon the trunks, all featuring a corpulent elf in rhinestone sunglasses forwardly thrusting his pelvis. The captions read "The Elvisking!" and "Elvisking Live!" and "Viva Las Valmar, Starring the Elvisking!"

"We must be in the realm of the Elvisking!" declared Sorkinshield, who had recently regained consciousness.

"I am a talking tree!" declared a Jerkwood tree. "Sorry. I forgot it was State the Obvious Day."*

"The Elvisking dwells yonder," continued Sorkinshield, "in a castle known as Graceland with his Elven Fangirls, who—"

Sorkinshield stopped his useless exposition abruptly, for a rich baritone voice began to flow through the forest like

_____

* You have to respect a forest that does not give up.

sweet molasses. Out from the trees leaped a horde of shrieking Elven Fangirls, wielding quill pens and baring body parts to be signed.

The Elven Fangirls' curvy figures suggested there might be food nearby, and even Sorkinshield, whose perception of women remained unchanged due to the fact that he hadn't interacted with any during any part of their adventure, thought these ladies were pretty cute.

As the Fangirls caressed them along, the mysterious song grew louder. Soon they approached Graceland's golden gates, engraved with the sheet music of a lost melody and the silhouette of a plump man catching his breath. At last they were led past the ivory pillars at the castle entrance and into the jungle-themed great hall.

It was there the Elvisking was sprawled upon a leopard-print throne, his enormous body clad in a gold-encrusted jumpsuit. Elven Fangirls styled his raven-black hair and massaged his pelvis with fingers dewed with rosewood oil and peanut butter. The Elvisking vaguely strummed a guitar with one hand; the other held a microphone to his pouty lips. The Little People marveled at the castle's size, grandeur, and utter lack of taste. Billy slipped on his anklet, incorrectly thinking that for once it might help him blend in with his surroundings.

After crooning the last verse of "You Ain't Nothin' but a Half-Elf," the Elvisking pointed a fleshy finger in the direction of the Little People. His demand was simple: "Whattarya . . . whoer these . . . wassup?"

"We are but poor travelers seeking shelter for the night," Sorkinshield replied. He elected not to disclose their intended destination. If the Elvisking learned of the treasure awaiting them, he might find it first, melt it down, and use it to sculpt a gold statuette of a baby angel playing a saxophone.

The King was unsure nonetheless. "I dunno, man, I think we gotta . . . darlin's, why dontcha throw 'em in the . . . we got dungeons, darlin's, babies . . . can't have no suspicious guys, no suspicions," he decreed.

With that, the Elvisking began a rendition of "Suspicious Guys." The few Elven Fangirls who had been trained to not scream or faint escorted all the YOLOers to Graceland's jailhouse. All, that is, except Billy.

With his anklet strapped back around his designated roll of fat, the wobbit again found that nobody could stomach to look at him. It wasn't that they couldn't see him—"No," thought Billy with a throaty chuckle, "that would have been silly!"—it was simply that no one could bear to look his way.

Suddenly Billy realized that this was no ordinary anklet, but a very special anklet, and quite possibly the one anklet to fool them all. It became immaculately clear to him the precise power the jewel brought to its wearer: to move at forty-eight frames per second, causing everyone around him to instinctively look away and vomit a little in their mouths.

Meanwhile, the Little People remained trapped in an especially chintzy dungeon. For days the Elvisking obstinately refused to free them, not even in exchange for Doc's promise to stop spitting out blood every time he saw gold lamé. Nonetheless, the imprisonment was surprisingly pleasant for the Little People. Every so often, the warden would throw a swinging party in the jailhouse, and Elven Fangirls would come down and dance with the Little People if the Elvisking was napping or in a coma. Ballin and Drawlin resisted at first (there were tales of old that spoke of the Elvisking stealing the Sound of Rock from their ancestors), but they eventually came to the conclusion that music was a universal language and appropriation could sometimes be an unfortunate but necessary step on the road to integration. Even Whorey, Slorey, and Kourtney got into the spirit of Graceland by losing touch with reality and rushing into doomed marriages with the warden.

At first Billy enjoyed any excuse to wear the anklet and make people physically ill, but he soon began to tire of life at Graceland. No one would look at him except for Doc, and only during his bouts of temporary blindness. He began to search for an escape, but the golden gate only opened up at the Elvisking's command. The King himself never found any reason to leave, so Billy slept in the fur-lined front seat of the Elvisking's hot-pink carriage.

But the wobbit soon discovered something peculiar, and was almost embarrassed to not have noticed it several days ago. In the middle of the tropical great hall was a vast indoor waterfall, and Billy decided to follow its stream in search of its source. Sure enough, like all rivers, it went directly through a cellar before meandering down to the Jerkwood forest. All Billy had to do was free the Little People and they could let the river carry them away from Graceland.

That night Billy silently waited for the warden to leave the jailhouse after a Cold War–themed party. When he finally emerged—obliviously humming "(Now and Then There's) A Troll Such as I"—Billy crept up from behind him and smashed him across the head with a platinum record. He then kicked the warden around with his stolen pair of the Elvisking's Suede Shoes of Sapphire, lifted his keys, and ran him over with the pink carriage. It was the perfect crime; it looked exactly like every other drunken night in Graceland.

In the jailhouse, Billy found the Little People still recovering from the last orgiastic rager. They had many questions, such as what his plan was, where they were, and if he could please try to be a little quieter. "No time now!" hushed the wobbit. "If the Elvisking wakes up and finds out how much of his peanut butter I ate tonight, we are done for!"*

As they left the jailhouse, Billy kindly returned the keys to the warden. "That will save him some of the trouble he is in for," said Billy to himself, placing the keys on the elf's bruised, viciously beaten, unconscious body.

The fugitives arrived at the cellar without impediment. The Elven Fangirls were all preoccupied, for the Elvisking had been in the bathroom for a really, really long time.

Though unable to look Billy in the eyes, Sorkinshield smiled in admiration. "Bagboy," he said, "walk and talk."

They headed in a circle around the cellar.

"I'm impressed," continued Sorkinshield. He stopped in his tracks. "That is all."

Billy showed the Little People the river that would deliver them out of Graceland.

"Bagboy, you worthless scoop of lard," snapped Sorkinshield. "I thought you had a sensible plan for how to escape!"

"Very well!" said Billy, downcast and rather annoyed. "Come along back to the jailhouse and I will lock you all in again, and you can discuss alternative plans over feasts and

---

* Billy ate all of the Elvisking's peanut butter that night, as "all of" is really the only acceptable serving size for a wobbit.

alcohol until you are all too drunk and bloated to ever escape!" This thought made Beefer and Buffer scream and reflexively start doing pull-ups. Everyone agreed it would be best to find some way to sail down the river.

There was not much available to them in the cellar, only a nuclear bunker, an armory, a time machine, and a pile of barrels. With no other choice, Billy and the Little People latched onto the time machine and floated with it down the river.

Poor Little People! The trip was tough for all, with the time machine constantly dunking them underwater and interrupting Sorkinshield's speeches. Kourtney frantically reapplied her makeup while Whorey and Slorey attempted to straighten their hair before the paparazzi could snap a photo. The ordeal reignited Beefer and Buffer's long-standing debate over whether or not swimming was just running for wet people.* Kiwi seemed annoyed, probably because time machines are not its natural habitat. But then Fili's keen eyes spotted an extraordinary rake within a barricaded fortress.

"Paddle toward it!" ordered Sorkinshield. "We have reached Rake-town!"

"What sort of creatures inhabit Rake-town?" Billy asked.

"Men," answered Sorkinshield. "Real men. Capable men. The sort of men I like. And their leader, Richard Nixon, will surely give us food and shelter." Like the Elvisking, Richard Nixon had more than once faked his own death in order to get a fresh start in Widdle Wearth.

The river flowed into Rake-town through a water gate in the barricade known as the Dryportal.

---

* It's not.

"Open up your water gate!" Sorkinshield bellowed at the guards.

"It's called a Dryportal," corrected the captain, but he complied. The guards of Rake-town were not keeping very careful watch, since there hadn't been any real need, what with Nixon's outstanding foreign policy record.

Men were not known to have particularly good food (and it remained a mystery how they grew the canned apparatuses they stored it all in), but Billy and the Little People welcomed the chance to see the town's famous Rake, which was enshrined in the town square. For what a tool it was! Its tines were arranged in the shape of a scallop shell too perfect to exist in nature, with ends curved like a baby's first smile. Leaves were said to quiver at the sight of the Rake's razor-sharp teeth, and then thank the heavens that such a magnificent foe should bring their demise. It was just a really solid rake, all things considered.

The Rake aside, there was nothing remarkable about Rake-town. Every house was the same shade of white, and Billy and the Little People guessed that Nixon dwelled in the largest of the white houses.

"Take us to your master!" Sorkinshield commanded the guard at the entrance, who was even more totally checked out than the captain at the Dryportal.

But the leader of Rake-town did not receive his guests cordially. "Gentlemen, you listen here and you listen good," he groused. "I'd sure like to know who you are and what gives you the right to make me late for my table-tennis practice."

Blood rushed to Sorkinshield's face. "I am Aaron Sorkinshield, leader of the Little People!" he shouted. "We are on a

YOLO to acquire Puff the Magic Dragon's treasure. We have defeated armies of trolls, Moblins, and a really big spider. We only just escaped the lair of the Elvisking. Dick, you know what I think? I think you're a small man. I think I could buy your Ping-Pong room and make it into a Ping-Pong room for orphans! I'm better than you! How dare you treat me like other people!"

Nixon glanced at a framed picture on the wall of him shaking hands with the Elvisking after a gentlemanly game of Who Can Sweat the Most? As he contemplated the risk of a rift with the king, Billy let out a large sneeze. Now, as I have tried to convey, the power of the anklet would make the fairest elf performing the loveliest dance in gorgeous midsummer look like the homeliest troll performing the thoroughest nose-picking in slushy late winter, so you can imagine what a wobbit sneezing might look like.*

"Look, Bagboy," said Sorkinshield as he looked away and gritted his teeth, "just take off that anklet, all right?"

When Billy sheepishly slipped it off, a young servant of Nixon's gasped. "Master!" he exclaimed. "It's the bagboy!"

"The what?"

"The bagboy! You know, the one we're always singing about, when we're not singing about the Rake!"

The citizens of Rake-town fell into two categories—the Silent Majority and the Always Singing Minority. Nixon had become accustomed to tuning out minorities, but this time he listened to what the young man had to sing:

---

* If you purchased one of the *Lampoon*'s 3D-Hologram-O-Books, scratch here until you see a wobbit sneezing in front of you:

The king of flimsy plastic,
The king of paper strong,
Although he may look spastic,
He'll fill our hearts with song.

Our kitchens will be refilled,
The shelves will be reracked,
He will clean up where we've spilled,
His change will be exact.

Although the line is growing,
He's patient with old men;
He'll ask them, "How's it going?"
As they search for a pen.

Your bags he'll always carry,
However much you take;
He'll make us all so merry,
Though much less than the Rake!

There were more verses to the song, but they were all about the Rake. Nixon, who had worked as a bagboy in his father's grocery, recognized an opportunity to tout his humble beginning and curry favor with the Always Singing Minority. Billy and his fellow YOLOers were thus sheltered in the second-largest white house and decked in respectable Republican cloth. Citizens and foreigners from far and wide asked Billy to bag their produce for them, though that was thought of as something to do after you'd seen the Rake. The Little People began to act a bit more kindly toward Billy, knowing how important it was to respect the layered metaphors of the many songs in this book.

At the end of a fortnight, the Little People began to think of departure. Nixon was not at all sorry to let them go. "I hope that dragon fries those freeloading sons of midgets!" he was heard to grumble on tapes released many years later. But all he said in public was, "You take care, now! Watch out for Puff!"

Before they left, Billy and the Little People beheld the Rake for one last time. They then looked up and to the left, and saw for the first time the Mountain with Zero Friends.

IX

Ready to Roughhouse

Billy pointed a fat wobbit finger at the great, pitiful-looking mountain in the distance. "What are we waiting for? Let's get over—*ouch!*" Billy had stepped on the rake and sent its handle flying into his face in a classic and hilarious blunder. They all laughed at the brief moment of levity in this deathly serious YOLO.

As they drew nearer to the mountain, they saw that there was nothing to see anywhere. Its surface, devoid of all life, looked *super lame*. The rake was maybe fifty times cooler, and that rake wasn't even on the Top Ten Coolest Rakes in Widdle Wearth list Slorey had been reading for the past five months. The list was twenty sentences long and Slorey could read about a sentence a week if she was really pushing herself. It took Whorey but four months to calculate this.

The closer they came, the more the group was dismayed by the Mountain with Zero Friends. Normal features of a Widdle Wearth mountain it had not: Where was the world-class ski resort? The commemorative mountain goat tours?

The thousands of St. Bernard dogs roaming around looking for
somebody to heal with their lifesaving medicine neck barrels?*
Why did everything smell vaguely of cauliflower? Who, pray
tell, would possibly want to spend any time here, considering
the Mountain of Four Thousand Three Hundred and Sixty-
seven Friends was close enough nearby that you could just
make out the laughter and snowmobile noises?

In truth the Mountain with Zero Friends wouldn't have
known itself why anybody bothered with it. It was a fluke
mountain to begin with, you see—just showed up one day
where once there was the Totally Amazing Valley. The men
of Fail avoided getting close to the mountain, just because it
wasn't their kind of mountain, you know, nothing personal. The
Little People originally only hung around there to play its Nin-
tendo 64 on single player and eat all the Cheetos it gave them.

They felt guilty saying it, but Billy and the Little People
felt uncomfortable around this mountain. It kept awkwardly
avalanching everywhere they tried to walk, and then it would
just make it worse with an apology avalanche. Kourtney tried
to hug the mountain out of pity, but it got her entire outfit utterly soaked, and not even in a flattering way. Fili was trapped
under an avalanche for about two weeks, until somebody noticed he was missing. Ballin got so fed up he screamed, "This
is so pathetic!" then felt bad about it and promised to go see a
movie with the mountain at some point. (I mention this only
because it is illustrative of the many comments made by Ballin
and Drawlin that could have been made by anybody, and are

---

* The creator of the accidental spell that created millions of St. Bernards through-
out Widdle Wearth hasn't come forward, but everyone's pretty sure it was Dumbledalf.

certainly more emblematic of a universal range of emotions than that of any one race or ethnicity. It's important to note that if I keep bringing up Ballin and Drawlin's angry comments, it is only because this a long and difficult YOLO and if I was to record all they said and did, this would probably need to be a trilogy. If, for example, the only comment Drawlin makes in this chapter happens to be about the infamous Widdle Wearth race riots, that does not mean we can reduce to him a stereotype of a Little Person who is always harping on nothing but race riots. I, for one, do no such thing, and neither should you.)

"I bet this mountain was too aloof to even take a side during last summer's race riots," Drawlin remarked.

It was in between losing Fili and remembering that Kiwi had a brother when they realized they had a long search for the secret door ahead of them, or to the left or right of them, depending. It could have been inside that nasty cavern that was next to that other nasty cavern. Or it could have been beneath the Stinky Cliff that was next to the Stinky in a Different Way Cliff. But first our travelers thought they should check out what was at the front of the line of Widdle Wearthlings snaking down the side of the mountain. In Widdle Wearth, lines rarely formed in front of secret doors, but you never knew. And there was the fact that Dumbledalf had been inviting everyone he met to the secret door since the beginning of the YOLO.

Still, the line was unusual. Billy had been the first to spot it, exclaiming, "Wow, a line! I love lines!"

This was true. Billy had spent his whole life looking out at lines of customers waiting for him to bag their fine groceries. He had always wondered what it was like to be in line. Maybe lines were how you met women? Billy would soon find out.

After the first three weeks of waiting in line, they could make out at the distant front a massive rock, and in front of that a velvet rope and a bouncer in cool-as-Sorkinshield shades. He was clearly a winner of a man—emotionally and intellectually fulfilled, strong personal brand. Groin pointed out that the bouncer held a long rod, which excited all for what might come next from the prophetically audacious Little Person's mouth. But soon it was clear that it was just a baton to hit people with when he rejected them. And he rejected everyone: elves, Moblins, cool Humans who had cool catch-phrases like "That ain't nobody's Tabasco," various woodland creatures trying to build nests along the mountainside, indig-enous trees, and Dumbledalf at least five times. They kept try-ing to wave to Dumbledalf, but he was either pretending not to know them or having an episode of dementia.

Another month later they moved up a few places, but in a cool way. After four months they made it to the bouncer.

"No secret door here. Move along," he intoned. Then he raised his long rod, ready to strike.

"Wait!" shrieked Billy. "We waited for so long. Please. We're good Little People and a wobbit. We pay our taxes, we don't litter, none of us has ever kicked a dog, we all subscribe to the *Harvard Lampoon*, we've never committed arson—"

"Hold on. Did you say you subscribe to the *Lampoon*? The *Harvard Lampoon*? The oldest continually published humor magazine in the world?"

"Of course," said Billy. "We all know that the *Lampoon* is the most entertaining, insightful, and enriching achievement of letters in the history of the written word."

"You better not be joking," snapped the bouncer. "It's deadly serious when the *Lampoon* is involved. I'll check the list." He looked at a scroll of parchment rimmed in gold, a vague and beautiful light shining from it.

"Yup, you're right here: 'B. Bagboy and all his Little People Friends or whatever.' The twenty-dollar annual subscription plan, huh? Good choice. You guys can go in."

The bouncer knocked on the rock three times. Then he knocked sixteen more times, breathed really heavily on it a few times, and pressed his fingers against a keypad drawn with sidewalk chalk and whispered, "Beep boop boop beep." Then he put a bit of dynamite under the rock and set it off, exploding the rock into a thousand bits.

The bouncer pulled back the velvet rope. "Coat check to your right; no flash photography."

They walked in, following the thumping bass coming through the walls. Magic was everywhere. Magic walls that were not the color of dirt, magic urinals that automatically flushed, magic balls hanging from the ceiling, covered in reflectors and spinning silently, ominously, beautifully, as if by the dark magic of Moblin spells. It was by far the best club on the mountain.

But all that magic made the Little People nervous, and soon their beards were drenched in sweat, which can be a real hazard for Little People. Sorkinshield's great-granduncle had drowned in beard sweat during a nerve-racking first date. The Little People decided it was probably cooler anyway if they just stayed in the coat check.

Of course, someone had to be brave and bold and fearless, and the Little People figured the protagonist was the best person for the job. And so Billy started down the dark cavern into the mountain alone, wobbling with fright on top of his regular wobbling. The hall still possessed the remnants of the classic Little People style from when they called the mountain their home: big tufts of hair growing out of the walls, everything inexplicably covered in mud. The "Dragon This Way" neon signs would have been a real help if Billy had been able to read. But at least the graffiti wasn't that offensive, and Billy was impressed at himself for understanding the one reading "Gabe <3s Melissa" right above two hugging skeletons huddled on the ground.*

Billy kept on into the depthiest depths of the mountain, until there it was: the deepest chamber. It had a bathroom and a janitor's closet. He went back one level of depth and there it was: Magic Dragon. Puff. He had so many names.† The awful dragon looked exactly like the songs described him. Horrifyingly woeful eyes, iridescent green scales of death, tufts of hair around his ears that looked like cotton candy—*poisonous* cotton candy. What's worse, he was fast asleep. He clutched five or six teddy bears and a ream of paper on which he had written "JACK." "Probably dreaming some psychologically troubling evil dragon dreams," thought Billy. "Probably dismembering some unicorns in his dreams. Probably performing hate crimes and stealing food from old ladies." Oh, he was so steamed. That dragon was going to be so dead when somebody else killed him later.

But then he saw the spoils. *"Ay, caramba,"* Billy tastefully quoted. It was incredible. There must have been sixty thousand

---

* It was probably better that Billy couldn't understand some of the less helpful wall writing, such as "Saruman <3s Sauron, Who Is Such a Babe," and "Dumbledalf Is Looking for a Dog Named Serious."
† Often Puff imagined what nicknames friends would give him if he had friends. Like: Puffy, Puffster, Mr. Puff, Tough Puff, uff, ff, P-Dragon, and the Beloved Dragon with No Companions.

trophies, and that was just the Oscars. There were another ten thousand Grammys, a slew of People's Choice Awards, a huge pile of MTV Video Music Awards, no BET Awards, and a single Tony Award for Best Lighting Design.

Billy smiled. This was going to be easier than making an elf cry. All he had to do was ankletize himself into forty-eight fps and stuff some Emmys into his fat rolls. Goodness knows he had enough of those to carry home HBO's entire trophy case. Billy squeezed on his anklet and rolled some of his leg fat down to his feet for extra padding. Utter silence would be necessary to carry this caper off successfully. "It's like I'm back in Wobbottabad, bagging potato chips without being allowed to make a single sound or else I instantly get burned to death," he said to himself. He clasped his hands over his mouth. He should have thought it to himself.

Puff awoke with a start. He rose up, yawned, rubbed his eyes, brushed his teeth, and looked all around him. He wore a homemade T-shirt that said "Hug Me, I'm a Normal Dragon!"

What was a poor wobbit to do? Billy threw a Golden Globe at him.

"Is somebody there?" asked Puff, because being a Magic Dragon means you can speak the same English that every single other creature in Widdle Wearth speaks (though the Jerkwood forest spoke it with an offensive Mexican accent). "If this is that one rude water buffalo again, or that insult-slinging wizard, I will inform the authorities immediately." Puff stuck out his snout, not unlike a dog's nose except for 685 times bigger.

"But wait. You smell like . . . like a friend! Oh boy, oh boy."

Billy thought for a moment. He had to be careful about this. Dragons were capable, presumably, of killing wobbits.

"So . . . how are things?" Billy patted himself on the back. He could not believe how good he was at making conversation.

"I'm great now that you're here, buddy! My insides have warmed right up." Puff's insides, a mixture of pretty clouds and endangered dolphin sanctuaries, had won a few People's Choice Awards themselves in the last age.

"That's great," said Billy. "Great." He knew not how to proceed. This was usually the part of a wobbit conversation when everybody would break to either eat doughnuts or breathe out of their mouths for a while. The dragon would surely devour him if he did not act quickly. He'd sucked his thumb enough to know he tasted delicious.

But Puff was already making the next move, tossing a giant, crudely welded ring of trophies at Billy.

"Have a friendship bracelet!" roared the dragon in his bloodcurdlingly beautiful voice. "We. Are. Now. Besties!"

Billy was rather sure he had just survived an attempted murder, but standard policy was to give every dragon a second chance, so he stuck around. Still, he decided he might as well hurry up and start stuffing trophies into his skin crevices while the distracted dragon rambled on about the various tortures he would put Billy through.

"I have so much planned for us—maybe we could do origami together later today? Then I have a couple of tickets to a sing-along screening of *Suddenly Moblin: The Musical*, but if you'd rather, we could do a pub crawl or just stay in and weave baskets. And we should definitely sign up for a cooking class! I'm so excited! Jack won't do any of this stuff with me." The dragon held up the ream of paper labeled "JACK." "Listen, keep this between you and me, but I worry Stack of Paper

Named Jack and I have gotten really distant. I think it might be that one time I accidentally lit him on fire."

There was now no denying that Puff wanted to kill him, be it a quick death by fire or a slow death through ordeal. Billy could barely contain his fear, and for a wobbit that meant more uncontrollable wobbling.

"Ooh," said Puff, "I smell you getting closer. I think somebody wants to cuddle!"

Billy was petrified. He was wobbling like a pendulum now, and was very weighed down by the awards, especially the Grammys, which seemed to be made of pewter. But just then the dragon stopped.

"Wait," Puff said bravely. "I just want to warn you that dragons aren't necessarily the optimal cuddlers, with our hard scales and very tiny arms and the fire we breathe, so I really need you to be supportive and not make fun of me while I'm trying to cuddle, okay?"

But as Puff was saying this, Billy took his chance and ran, awards spewing out of his massive frame left and right, clanging to the ground, sending sparks flying everywhere, lighting parts of Puff's bed and couch on fire. "I am a hero and heroes cannot die!" cried Billy. "And I will bag various canned goods and fresh produce well into old age, just as I prophesied to myself once!"

Puff didn't understand why his friend was running away, and for a harrowing moment he doubted himself. Maybe Magic Dragons never got to have friends. Maybe you had to trade in friends when you acquired fire-breathing powers and the ability to fly and wisps of immortality. Maybe that wasn't even a terrible trade-off, especially compared to the sentient swamp lumps from the Sad Lands, who could have all the friends they wanted as long as they were other sentient swamp lumps from the Sad Lands. But Puff only wavered long enough to change into his "I'm Puff and I'm Rough, So Let's Roughhouse" shirt. Then, full of a new lust for friendship, he burst out of the mountain, frolicking in friendly furor, blowing horribly destructive fireballs of joy. Meanwhile, the Mountain with Zero Friends stayed sadly behind, though it had always been ready to be Puff's BFF. This irony was lost on both, because irony didn't exist in Widdle Wearth.*

Billy rushed posthaste back to the Little People, who had been sitting in complete silence at the coat check. Not a thing had happened, save for a brief make-out session between Drawlin and Kourtney in the corner, and both had quickly realized it would affect their professional relationship. Kiwi also hooked up with Loin, but that had been happening for months.

Billy explained everything to the Little People and urged them to explore the mountain while Puff was away. So the Little People at last set off for the second-deepest chamber. And when they saw the various television and media awards, they practically ripped their beards off with joy. Everybody hooted and hollered, and they could finally use all that heavy confetti they'd packed.

After a couple of hours of partying, they started exploring the treasure, and that's when Billy spotted it. A bald gem, gruff and endearing, full of wisecracks. It was the Alan Arkinstone, he was sure, and he knew it was Sorkinshield's greatest desire to possess this roughly handsome, award-winning stone with

---

* Irony would later become the most important weapon ever wielded by anybody. Like most magical things, irony was invented by the *Harvard Lampoon*.

expert comedic timing. He stuffed it into the globule space right below his anklet, where he knew no one would want to look.

Eventually they grew bored of the Oscars, which were mostly for Best Makeup anyway, and decided to get out of the mountain for a while. Sorkinshield knew the most efficient route, past the food court and the spa and the official gift shop, to the great front gates with a dragon-shaped hole where Puff had broken through earlier that day. They gazed out over the sad, sad mountain, realizing that all the golden accolades in the world were nothing compared to that feeling of finally returning to your one true home. They got bored and depressed within five minutes.

X

How to Desolate Your Dragon

Now if you wish, like the Little People, to learn what happened to Puff the Magic Dragon, you must go back to the day when he stormed out of the Mountain with Zero Friends. Luckily, this is the same day just described in that last chapter, so it's not going to take a whole lot of effort from either of us.

At the time, the men of Rake-town were mostly indoors—and you would be too if it was cold! The women, possibly due to weather, were nowhere to be found.

Little could be seen of the Mountain with Zero Friends from Rake-town, as the River That Ran Water blocked its lower base and nobody wanted to look at an awkward loner for too long anyway. It was an age of swift and rather exciting evolutionary progression, and sympathy was a weakness in the battle for survival. It is said the great apes only managed to acquire opposable thumbs because they could never figure out how to truly love one another. I do not know who said this. To be honest, I doubt he was a scientist.

And so the residents of Rake-town devoted little attention to the Mountain with Zero Friends. It was certainly no help that all that was up there was a deadly dragon who wore the most tiresome T-shirts. The Humans could only make out the utmost peak of the mountain from their point of view, and they were pretty bad at viewing matters from any other perspective.

Even so, they could not help but notice a flash of gold atop the mountain on that fateful night. There was much discussion among the Rakers as to what might be the source.

"Perhaps it is the Little People, sending gold down the river. The songs are coming true at last."

"Unlikely," said a grim man. "If you found gold, would you immediately throw it into a river?"

The men glanced around nervously. None had considered this before. The edicts of the songs were a little impractical upon closer examination. Also problematic was the fact that the lyricist had drowned six hundred years ago from paranoid delusions of river treasure.

"We've been deceived by the tunes," one realized.

"It is true," said another. "The tunes are just so catchy."

"Then hear my tune," said the grim man, growing grimmer. He stood and belted out a jingle three octaves lower than even an elven bass clarinet could go.

Na Na Na Na Na Na Na Na Na
Na Na Na Na Na Na Na Na Na
Bard the Batman!

The grim man's name, you see, was Bard the Batman, and the *na na na*'s were shameless filler.

Just then a golden streak shot down the river from the north, lighting up the nighttime sky.

"It's a bird!"

"It's a plane!"

"When did we invent planes?"

Bard shook his head.

He climbed into his Bardmobile and sped off to the white-washed home of Richard Nixon.

"Mr. Nixon-in-Chief, listen to me. Either the dragon is coming, or I'm not some ordinary billionaire."

"You're not an ordinary billionaire," guessed Nixon obliviously.

"This is no time for backstories. Call our men to arms! Cut the bridge!"

Nixon leaned back in his swivel chair and placed his feet upon his desk. At the time, it seemed like the pinnacle of power—but as you will soon see, Nixon had a lot to learn about chairs.

"Riddle me this," Nixon said gruffly. "If it's a dragon that can fly, why would I cut the bridge?"

"I have heard of such Riddlers, and I am not in the mood for games." Bard grimaced. Bard was never in the mood for games. He was usually in the mood for either brooding or tending to his many bats.

"If we cut the bridge, then we can't escape, and we would trap ourselves on an island with a dragon and die."

"Don't overthink it," said the Batman, no less grimly than his previous grimness.

"How does destroying our own bridge help us at all?"

"Because if we don't destroy our bridge, the dragon will *destroy* our bridge!"

Nixon immediately understood this perfect logic.

"Cut the bridge!" he roared to his security team, the Gossipy Service.

Suddenly the warning trumpets sounded three staccato blows. One blow meant rivers running with gold, two blows meant somebody acquired a new trumpet they were proud of, three meant public dragon attack, and four meant it was going to rain tomorrow. After waiting around a few moments hoping there would be a fourth blow, everybody fled their homes, shrieking in anguish as the mighty dragon crooned above them:

Puff the Magic Dragon
Could grasp reality
And was not a delusional dragon
And made a normal amount of friends

I could go on, dear reader, but I'd rather not make you drop these pages in fright and get the Barnes & Noble employees mad at you.

As Puff swept over the rather forgettable lake alongside Rake-town's storied rake, his fiery puppy dragon eyes homed in on the one and only bridge. He headed down to cross it by foot, recognizing it as your standard symbolic bridge of friendship—but no! Just in the nick of time, the Humans blew up their only means of escape, saving themselves from having their bridge destroyed by a dragon.

As Bard watched his town come under attack, he was flummoxed by a moral quandary.* Time and again, no matter what

---

* Story of his life.

trouble seemed to strike down upon his beloved Rake-town, he was the only one brave enough to stop it. All the other residents were incredibly ignorant and idiotic and never appreciated his good deeds. Nonetheless, he did whatever was necessary to protect his town and its irascible mayor. He had only one arbitrary rule: never kill a dragon.

Bard, therefore, was terribly uncertain how to respond to the threat of the dragon. He now watched as Puff dove through the ravaged community, laying the land to waste, though it did cross his mind that grimness would come even more easily if his whole community was burned out of existence.

As soon as Puff saw the bridge of friendship crumble to the sea, the poor dragon could think only of his predictably sad youth in the slums of Widdle Wearth. It was there that Puff lived with his neglectful parents, two perennial underachievers who were dragons for a living. For centuries the storks were too afraid of the fire-breathing creatures to deliver any babies, and when they did, they often picked rather bad dragons to be parents. Puff's parents were the most dismal dragons in all of Widdle Wearth, isolating Puff from his peers and stunting his development as a socially productive member of the dragon community. There was nothing for Puff to do to pass the days in his dark and lonely cave but watch reruns of *Bay, oh Wulf!*, an award-winning saga about being a wolf that instilled Puff with his love for mantelpiece trophies. Had he been born a wolf, how marvelous life would have been! Wolves traveled in packs and always had friends at their side.* Dragons flew alone, and pretending that the clouds at their side were friendly cumulonimbus companions only worked for so long.

---

* Counterpoint: the lone wolf.

Seeing the Humans' refusal to forge the fires of friendship pushed Puff over the edge. He could not help himself; he did as you and I would do, and wept. Honestly, you and I would weep a lot if we lived in Widdle Wearth.

A dragon's tears are not like most other tears, however. Their happier tears turn into above-average jelly beans, but their saddest tears can light the ground afire. With each tear that trickled down the scales of Puff's face, another idyllic Rake-town gated community burst into deadly flames, with all the Lexus SUVs and high-end gas grills exploding in luxurious spectacle.*

One of these tears happened to land on Nixon's white house, razing the structure instantly. As the building toppled, Nixon fled straight for the Dryportal, desperately hoping to shield himself from any further damage. Some other unnamed people also died, and you should feel sad about that too.

Bard saw all of this carnage, but he was unmoved, and grim.

But then he saw the side mirror of his Bardmobile. A rogue piece of wood had been flung against it, leaving a minor but noticeable scratch that would take a good hour and a half to buff out.

This changed everything for Bard. He climbed into his Bardmobile and threw his morality code out the window, damaging his side mirror even more. He knew what he had to do. Driving ten miles per hour over the speed limit, he reached the nearest Bardmobile repair shop within minutes. He dropped off his car and waited for the mechanic to put out the fire all over his pants.

---

* Think CG effects.

While Bard waited, he looked around for anything that might help him defeat the dragon. With so much of the town burned, all that was left in the area was an armory, a nuclear bunker, and a time machine. As he tried to puzzle out a way to utilize these unutilizable objects, an old Baltimore Ravens line-backer tried to perch himself on Bard's shoulder. They both instantly toppled to the ground.

The Raven extended a hand and helped Bard up from the burning floor. "Huddle up now."

They thrust their arms around each other and lowered their heads.

"Listen," the Raven said, "you look like you're in a bit of a jam. Whenever me and my team were facing clothes-wearing, crying dragons on the field, coach would call for the old Blue-forty-two."

Bard frowned, and since his mouth was the only visible part of his face, it was rather clear how he was feeling. "I don't know that one," he grimmed.

The Raven pulled the huddle tighter and whispered around the area where he imagined Bard's ear to be beneath his mask. "The old Nuclear Bunker–Armory–Time Machine combo."

Bard grimmed noddingly.

"Break!" the Raven cawed. "Break down the barriers of space and time!" They exited the huddle and took their stances.

Bard sprinted down his route, circling around the nuclear bunker to lure Puff into a false sense of safety and cutting across to the armory to find some guns and such. The armory was all out of guns, but by shooting arrow after arrow at the end of Puff's tail, Bard herded the adorably friendless beast right through the time machine, sending Puff straight into the 1960s folk-rock movement. There Puff would live out his days alongside Fritos, Spam, and Gulf Oil barracks, all admittedly dated references that I apologize for. Even Richard Nixon, whose favorite book was the *Harvard Lampoon's Bored of the Rings*, had absolutely no idea what was going on.

The waxing moon was stripped bare of its hair in the twinkling sky. The thick fog smoldered through the hills, mixing with the smoke to create a layer of Smog, which, come to think of it, would have been another possible name for a dragon that wouldn't have been too bad in some sort of parody book, maybe with the dragon's conceit being that he terrorizes towns by emitting a toxic amount of pollution. But that would have made for an entirely different book that would have sold the exact same number of copies.

The debris scattered west toward the marshes of Jerkwood, and between the wails of the Race of Men, if you listened closely, you could hear the whispers of that forest as dusk lumbered toward dawn.

"Sucks for you," it said.

And so the Humans lamented the destruction of their town, though they were pretty pleased the one surviving building was the House That Everybody Liked. In the heat of the moment—temperatures were still around 120 degrees Fahrenheit—they felt a tremendous sense of loss, which felt a lot like having third-degree burns all over your limbs. But four out of five residents had survived the chaos, and the fifth that hadn't were largely concentrated in the town's dental school, which really was just asking for trouble with that flammable toothpaste they were developing. Most of their woods remained undamaged, and their pastures too. Of course, the cattle had now seen things, terrible things, so the milk would never taste the same, and the milkman had been incinerated,

terribly incinerated, so no one would ever notice the difference. But the dragon had left for an objectively more groovy
time and place, and everybody was just grateful they didn't
have to go to any folk-rock-movement YOLTs themselves.[*]
What's more, the dragon had left the Mountain with Zero
Friends completely unguarded. The Humans had not yet realized just what this meant. As I said, they were ignorant and
idiotic and were liable to forget to think about the insides of
mountains when their houses were burning down.

And there were other matters at hand. Word traveled
quickly across town that their Nixon-in-Chief had not acted so
chiefly in their time of need, though he did act very Nixonly. A
virulent mob found him on the shores of the Dryportal, stuck
in a life vest, calling for Pat to cut him out of the damn thing.
Nixon's cocker spaniel, Chess, was chewing on his left pant leg.

But now that Puff had gone to a better place, Nixon could
practically hear the Oscar acceptance speeches awaiting him
deep within the mountain.

"Hear me now," he said, waving the one hand that wasn't
caught in his vest. "I am not a crook."

"Lies!" cried a townsperson. "If only Bard the Batman had
not perished in the time machine doohickey. Now there was
an honest man, and a brave man, even if he had some troubling
mood issues sometimes."

"It is a shame he died," echoed another.

"Yes, a real shame," agreed a third. But this third man was
no ordinary third man—he stepped behind the podium and
pulled off his mask, revealing his bat mask beneath it! It was
the Batman!

---

[*] YOLT: You Only Live Twice.

"Bard is no longer dead. For I am he, Bard of the line of Grimion. I am the time-transporter of the dragon!"

"His story continues!" the Rakers cheered. "King Batman! King Batman!"

Nixon could plainly see that public opinion was shifting, and he still didn't know where Pat was with those damn scissors. Come to think of it, he hadn't seen her or any other women in years. He realized that he was okay with this.

"Now hold on," Nixon said, and the residents felt instantly inclined to forgive him, "but why is that I am to blame? Was it I who sent the dragon storming from the mountain down into our homes? I think not. Someone find a measuring stick, and you will see that I am tall enough to ride any roller coaster in Widdle Wearth. You know who isn't? Sorkinshield and his Little People! It is they who have wronged us in pursuit of their hordes of gold."

"Here, here!" the crowd cried. "We have been cheated by the Little People. The smallest shadows are the hardest to see."

As you can imagine, that immediately became a proverb.

"Now, I am the last person to call Bard the Batman anything other than an ordinary billionaire—I called him such not more than fifteen minutes ago. I am as thankful for his service as the rest of you, but Rake-town has no king, and I am your elected leader. Moments like this are what we ratified a constitution for, and populist anger like this is why I never let you read it. The line of Grimion were the lords of Fail, not Rake-town, which really stinks for you."

Fail was a destroyed town in Moblin territory that everyone once had high hopes for. It was widely accepted now as a pretty big fail.

"Fools!" said the Batman. "The Little People did not cheat

us. They were likely the first victims when Puff descended the mountain. Friendship is not a victimless crime."

The residents nodded solemnly. They did not understand what that meant, but it was probably another famous proverb.

"I am with you, Richard Nixon," said Bard. "United we stand, divided we stand too far apart to hear each other and work effectively as a team."

They would have to workshop that one before it became a proverb. "Nonetheless," cried a townsperson, "you have wronged us and you have lied to your town, Mr. Nixon. As such, we have no choice but to beseech you. We beseech you to be an honest man."

Everyone agreed that this was the best course of action, so Nixon was thenceforth beseeched by his people. Having taken part in such a momentous political act, the citizens of Raketown applauded and hugged one another. The nimble-handed managed both at once.

Then they looked upon the mountain in the distance, and the distance in the further distance, and the horizon at distance's end. It was so far just then, and yet—well, you should flip the page, because, boy, will you be surprised.

The crowd dispersed to gather arms and prepare for the fight ahead, singing once more of the golden river that was once again a real possibility.

Nixon raised his hands above his head and held out two fingers on each. He descended the podium's stairs. It instantly became a proverb.

XI

A Bildungsroman Moment

B ut back to Billy and the Little People. This story is not named *Richard Nixon and Also a Dragon*, though that probably would have sold more copies. After pulling an all-nighter watching forty years' worth of Academy Awards opening monologues, they still had no information about threats on the horizon or what the difference between sound editing and sound mixing was. There were many birds warming up outside the mountain, a startling array that spanned the spectrum from Hawks to Seahawks as the 2004 Baltimore Ravens roved between.

"Why are there so many birds?" asked Sorkinshield in an annoyed voice that demonstrated just how many birds there were. "What is this? A lecture on symbolism in Shakespeare? A Hitchcock movie? The sky?"

Before any of the Little People could prove him right, Billy leaped to his wobbling feet.

"It's Kyle Boller, the Ravens starting quarterback!"

The Little People were dumbfounded by the Raven's grace

under pressure, not to mention his glistening hair. Never before had they seen someone who could run a mile in an amount of time worth measuring. Yes, he looked like a man who could lift twice as much as Beefer and Buffer while listening to half as much Imagine Dragons.

"Better run the buttonhook again," Boller said to his receivers. He looked upon the mountainside, a draconian canvas pocked with magma pits and littered with skulls. "It's places like this that remind you the world really is nicer outside of Baltimore."

For over an hour the team practiced their hearts out, but it just wasn't coming together. There was palpable frustration as Beefer and Buffer jostled for autographs. Finally the Ravens took a Waterade break near the Little People.

"Here's what's gonna happen," said head coach Brian Billick, a brave warrior, though certainly no Andy Reid. "Kordell, we need you to be faster. Did you stop puffing the magic dragon?"

"I did, coach," said Kordell.

"They stopped the dragon!" misinterpreted Billy. And the Little People rejoiced. Many a chest was bumped that day.

"Shush," shushed Billy. "I need to hear what they're saying."

". . . and that's why they're gonna try to surround us!" screamed Billick. His linemen were not amused. "This is our house, and they're coming for it. They won't be afraid to grab these precious stones." His hands rested confidently on his waist.

"They're going to surround us. And they're coming for the treasure!" Billy mistranslated. And the Little People were terrified. Many a pair of pants was soiled that day.

Fili and Kiwi were rather confused by all the football, but a cricket metaphor put the situation into proper context for Fili, and Kiwi had found some crickets earlier that he was happily eating.

Alas, the Ravens stormed away to run some sprints, and Billy and the Little People were left alone again to speculate about the past, and the future, and whether there were any more time machines lying around that could mess with either of those.

Then the lights dimmed, and the music grew slow and dramatic. Sorkinshield began to speak:

"Look at us. A bunch of Little People stuck far away from home. Barely capable of walking here or there. Surrounded by Humans. Unsure of ourselves and our sexualities."

The Little People nodded their heads, glad someone had finally said it.

"But we *are* sure of some things, like that Fili and Kiwi share 99 percent of their DNA. Now what are we here to do, you ask? Well—would you mind?"

Doc stopped struggling to bandage the bleeding hand he'd injured doing cartwheels during the Ravens' practice. If you've ever tried to bandage one hand before with nothing but your other hand to do it, you know he looked hilarious.

"We're here to keep this treasure," Sorkinshield began again. "We didn't come all this way to come home poor, and we've already come home. All that's left is to sit here for as long as it takes for everybody else to get tired and leave. Now, who's with me?"

Beefer started a slow clap, and the others joined in, but it never sped up because they had literally been walking for months and were insanely tired.

"I think we should talk this through first," said Billy.

Sorkinshield gestured toward the Talking Corridor. He'd been lacking a Talking Corridor the entire YOLO, but now that they were back on Little People terrain, there was at last one at hand. Together he and Billy entered the figure-eight-shaped hallway, which enabled them to walk and talk forever or until the camera ran out of film.

"Look at my face," snapped Sorkinshield.

"Listen—" Billy started.

"Don't be ridiculous."

"But—"

"Does the great man settle for good?"

"I'm just saying—"

"Saying what?"

"Maybe we could—"

"Could what?"

"Aar—"

"Don't get cute with me."

"—on . . ."

"Listen, kid. I have two degrees from Harvard, one from Stanford, and a double doctorate from Oxford. I even have a master's degree in Listing Degrees from the Yale School of Dramatic Drama."

"P—"

"Do I think it's going to work?"

"le—"

"You bet your ass I do."

"ase—"

"Now let's get going!"

Sorkinshield exited the Talking Corridor, and all the Little People cheered. They vowed to work harder than they ever had at sitting in one place. But even though wobbits are perhaps Widdle Wearth's foremost experts in sitting, Billy did not share the Little Peoples' enthusiasm. He had an uneasy feeling in his gut, and he didn't think it was because of those Video Music Awards he'd eaten earlier.

The others began barricading the Mountain with Zero Friends, blocking it off from all outside contact. They were mostly just going through the motions, since everybody knew you didn't need to do much to keep people away from the Mountain with Zero Friends.

Billy checked his phone and, after laughing at some uproarious tweets from his favorite Twitter account, @harvardlampoon, read a tweet from one of the Ravens. It appeared that soon they would have reinforcements—Sorkinshield's more sociopathic cousin, Bain, was coming with an army. Bain's Little People came from a dark, cruel land, where all were trapped in a pit, from which the only means of escape was climbing out.

This made the Little People more confident, which meant only one thing. It was time to burst into a jazzy rap about their dear leader:*

> Inside the mountain we do fit,
> Though barely, when we squeeze a bit.
> With Sorkinshield, (our thighs congealed)
> Until they leave, here we will sit.
>
> He is a mighty leader when,
> With parable and wit and ken
> Sly jokes he cracks and heads he smacks,
> His Nielsen rating's close to ten.

---

* This one's long, so you can go ahead and skip the whole next page.

It hasn't always been this way,
Once laugh tracks ruled and steered the day;
But buddy cops, and slapstick flops,
Won't match when he has words to say.

Our Sorkinshield will have his fun;
But someday sagas must be done.
Yes, what to do when things are through?
He starts again at season one.

His stories tell of gall and guts,
Of presidents and kings he tuts
Until they fold, and leave the gold
We'll stay here with him on our butts.

But has his saga heard its knell?
Though unforeseen, till time does tell,
We'll never balk at walk-and-talk
And hearing politicians yell.

Inside the mountain we do fit,
Though barely, when we squeeze a bit.
With Sorkinshield, (our thighs congealed)
Until they leave, here we will sit.

The repeated refrain at the end was probably unnecessary, and Billy wasn't so sure of Sorkinshield's plan. He felt it relied rather heavily on monologues and finishing other people's sentences. But he waited with the rest of them until the next day. Then, sure enough, something else happened.

From over the horizon came a flood of Humans. Humans

of every shape and size, though most of them were roughly human-size. It turns out that these Humans were on their way to a fantasy convention, where they would play make-believe as people in another universe. It was called CommaCon, because they would obsess over the most mundane details of life in an alternate reality, like how to properly use the Oxford comma and how not to badly split infinitives. They played at being actuaries and pediatricians instead of the usual boring archers and blacksmiths they had to be in real life. They had vivid and grotesque fantasies about paying a graduated income tax.

Then came the next wave of Humans, and it is this wave with which our YOLO is concerned. These Humans did not have the leisure of getting to attend fantasy conventions as traveling salesmen; they'd all been shafted with tedious day jobs where they fought to the death for honor and glory and revenge.

Forward stepped the commander of their forces, though carefully so as not to reveal his front side. Then he swirled around, sending his cape aflutter. Everyone gasped.

"Bard the Batman!" cried Sorkinshield.

"No," Bard said grimly, "I am just an ordinary billionaire. I drive a very normal-person car. It is called a Honda Civic. I know that my girlfriend loves me for my money, and not for my superpowers. But today I am here because I want you to surrender this mountain." And so the two began an exchange of informed dialogue.

"I cannot do that," said Sorkinshield.

"You can too," argued Bard.

"Can not."

"Can too."

"Can not."

All the Little People sat as hard as they possibly could. Their resolve would be an inspiration for generations to come. It was as if they had been born for this (or, in Doc's case, still-born for this).

"All right," said Bard, walking back to his Honda Civic. Everyone waited in suspense.

"What now?" asked Billy.

"I don't know," said Sorkinshield. "I've never ended anything on a clif

Later, the Little People grew tired from all the sitting and came to the conclusion it was time to lie down. They agreed to take turns guarding their food supply. Billy and Doc went first because nobody liked either of them. Everyone else got out their blankies and adorable Little Person nightcaps and went to sleep.*

How was the poor wobbit ever going to get home at this rate? Sitting got them nowhere. He couldn't die in this mountain. Perhaps another mountain on another day, but this one would make for the most awkward eternity ever. He had to act—and I mean really act, not just string together a bunch of overworded retorts.

"Hey, Doc, could you stare uninterrupted at that wall for about five hours?" asked Billy.

"Wouldn't be the first time," chuckled Doc.

"Great," said Billy. "It's for no particular reason."

---

* If you are picturing the Little People of *Snow White,* know that you are doing a great job making images in your head while you read. Keep up the good work.

As Doc privately celebrated his very first words of the book, Billy smuggled the Arkinstone into one of his kangaroo pouches and slipped on the anklet, transforming into a forty-eight fps nausea-inducing blunder. He slid through an emotional crack in the Mountain with Zero Friends—a weakness for rhubarb pie, like its mother used to make—and landed on a conveniently placed trampoline, where he bounced for the better part of an hour.

After he broke the trampoline, he sneaked past the guards of the opposing forces. They were followers of the Elvisking, and were naturally too busy arguing about where they should have their bodies signed to notice another body entering the fray.

But after spotting the nearby stream, the wobbit could not help but splash around and try to rid himself of the mountain's stench.

"Wait a minute," said an Elven Fangirl. "That water flying through the air for no particular reason is giving me a headache."

They realized somebody was in the water, and they took to him like their idol took to fame-induced depression. They hauled Billy to captivity, needing a full harem to carry him through the camp. The wobbit did not put up a fight. He only asked for soap.

When they set him down in a makeshift tent, he updated his list of requests.

"I am Billy Bagboy, companion of Aaron Sorkinshield, and I wish to speak to your king." The Elven Fangirls wondered how exactly this massive, doughy fellow could possibly be a companion of a Little Person. But some of the wobbit's more charismatic fat globules reminded them of the Elvisking's fat globules, so they took him to where the King held court. Bard the Batman was, thankfully, also there, because Billy was doubtful that the Elvisking could use his mouth to make words these days.

"What do you want?" asked Bard, in a tone so low that only nearby dolphins could hear.

"I am here to try to make peace."

"That's big talk from a little man," Bard answered, in a booming bass that reset all of the cell phones in the room. The Elvisking gently gyrated his hips.

"Well, I mean it," said Billy, instinctively lowering the pitch of his own voice.

The Elvisking gyrated faster, with more bravado, and in a way that implied the beginning of the end of a racially segregated society.

"Here," said Billy, pulling out the Arkinstone. "Sorkinshield values this very much, and I'm sure he'd listen to you if you had it to bargain with."

The Elvisking and Bard marveled at the magnificent gem, resplendent in its gritty authenticity and likable personality.

"Why would you do this?" asked Bard, looking at the night sky. The Elvisking played a blues-influenced chord progression on his acoustic guitar while puckering his lips.

Billy shrugged. He was simply ready for his YOLO to be over, even if he'd only do it once.

"I cannot thank you enough," said Bard in a voice low and grim enough to cause hairline fractures in the teeth of everyone in the room. "But once is enough for now."

"I really appreciate it, you know—" Billy started, but he turned around to find that Bard and the Elvisking had both disappeared, even though they were on a platform in the middle of an empty field. He kicked himself for having spoken to them facing the wrong direction in the first place and ventured off toward the shining light of the Humans' capital.

Hours later, Billy arrived at the Coliseum of Representatives, just as Congress was being called into session. It was a marvelous building filled with peanut vendors and spilt beer.

Billy watched as Richard Nixon banged his gavel for forty-five consecutive minutes. Eventually, the Red team and the Blue team stopped yelling at each other and the last air horn was silenced.

"All right. The first order of business is peace with the Little People." The air horns resumed, and a call-and-response of vuvuzelas began inside the stadium. It was not long before an elderly member of the Blue team had to be rushed out on a gurney and everyone settled down.

"We'll open up the floor," declared Nixon. The trapdoor built into the speaking floor swung wide open, revealing a goodly number of alligators. "I recognize the Congressman from East Ohiowa." And so it began.

"Gentlemen, I'll be bamboozled if we can't at least talk peace with our Little People here."

"Peace? With those small-bearded bumpkins?" chimed in a Red Pinnie. Yells came from all sides.

"Why are they so little?"

"What is this Arkinstone, anyhow?"

"To the gentleman from East Ohiowa, I say this: my people want peace of mind. They want a piece of the pie."

"We need a pie that everyone can have a slice of."

"An equal slice? Even Little People?"

"The size of the slice, my friends and colleagues, is immaterial to the matter at hand. What, pray tell, about the quality? My county, Thogam City, has the best pizza in all of Widdle Wearth, and I wouldn't swap my own mother for any other slice."

"Well if it's a pizza pie, who gets a say in the toppings? I like mushroom, but maybe the gentleman from Mississouri don't like mushroom. Maybe he wants Hawaiian."

"Pepperoni is good."

"Well, shoot. Let's get pepperoni."

"Okay, so maybe two pepperoni, two cheese. Is that enough?"

"Throw in one veggie, maybe?"

"No. Every time we order that, nobody winds up eating it. How about peppers and onions?"

"Fine. I'm dialing. Two cheese, two pepperoni, one peppers and onions."

"Hold on. Do we want mozzarella sticks?"

"I love me some mozzarella sticks."

"All right. Hi, is this Pizza Hovel? Yes, we'd like five pizzas: two cheese, two pepperoni, one peppers and onions. And an order of mozzarella sticks. And plates and napkins. Twenty-five minutes? Okay. Thanks."

The Congressmen paused for a moment of silence. Then they went back to the difficult and slow work of hammering out a workable piece of legislation.

An hour later they had not even mentioned the peace treaty. Billy grabbed ten or so slices of pepperoni to go and sneaked back toward the Mountain with Zero Friends.

Suddenly from behind a rock, out wandered Dumbledalf.

"Look at you, Hairy. Hardly a boy, hardly a man."

"I am fifty years old," said Billy.*

"You have to be careful of Necromorts," Dumbledalf warned him. "And also Filipinos."

"All right, then," said Billy, stepping away.

"Touch my head, boy," Dumbledalf whispered. "Take my secrets."

---

* I was shocked too.

XII

The Coolest Part!

The next day the wind shifted west, and we all know what that means.

Meanwhile, the lands below the Mountain with Zero Friends filled with forces upon forces, racking up more friend requests in a matter of hours than the mountain had ever known. Worried about appearing desperate, the mountain played it coy, leaving all requests pending, so nobody was quite sure of who was friends with whom.

Then Bain at last arrived, come to the aid of the Little People, brother in arms to Sorkinshield and cousin in genetics because of a drunken and regret-filled night Bain's granduncle had with Sorkinshield's oldest aunt.

Bard the Batman would not let Bain pass round the eastern bend; east was one of the four directions, and goodness knows you have to remember them all. Billy marched forth with Bard to speak with Bain to see if there could be a peace that might prevent the need for any sequels.

"From whence come you?" asked the Batman in his deep bass, grim as ever.

"I am Bain, son of Inane, son of Pain," said Bain, son of Inane, son of Pain. He spoke grimly, with a pitch deep enough to ruin a baby's whole day. "We are hastening to my kinsmen in the mountain, who have sent word of a casting call for a gritty thriller set on the stage of a sports news show. Why do you stand here as though you wish to kill me so?" It was the polite thing to say in such a situation, though it really meant, "Why do you stand here?"

"We stand here defending morality," said the Batman, more grimly and deeply than ever before.

"Is that so?" said Bain, one-upping the Batman in the grim lowering of his voice.

"It is so," said the Batman, going down the grimmest of octaves. Up by the mountain, Doc was having more aneurysms than usual.

"So?" reiterated Bain, flexing his grim vocal cords as wide as they could vibrate, struggling to utter the word.

"So," the Batman echoed, grunting with grimness so low that none could be sure he had even said it. Dead birds began falling from the sky.

"Hhhgrh," countered Bain, going grimmer and deeper than any in Widdle Wearth had ever gone before.

"Hrhhghh," went the Batman, his voice cracking with a grimness so deep it set fire to most of the Little People's hair.

And so it came to pass that neither could produce another audible sound. The two great leaders had no choice but to stare each other down with their tongues hanging out and their mouths open wide.

There was no getting around it. A fight was at hand—and at the YOLO's climax! Due to the definition of the word "climax"!

Each side prepared their forces, making sure to give their warriors one final lesson on how to miss with all their arrows until the very last one.

Yet just as the CG effects were about to get nifty, a swirling darkness overcame the sky above.

"Halt!" cried Dumbledalf. "Brooms swarm the sky."

Elves and Little People alike stopped in their tracks and watched with great confusion.

"Those are just bats," said Bard the Batman, grimly relieved. "I was wondering where I'd left them. Alas! They bring word of a Moblin attack. They come upon wargis to possibly avenge the possible death of Tony Moblin."

"Come, everyone!" said Dumbledalf. "A Wizarding Tournament! I am a wizard!" He laughed heartily, then grew incredibly sad. "Do come now, or we shall all die immediately."

And so the Batman and Bain and Billy and everybody else I haven't bothered to describe in proper detail gathered round, and hence were drawn the lines in the Battle of the Five Armies. It was the Moblins and the wargis on one side, and then also the Elves and the Little People and the Humans. Five-ish armies. Close enough.

And so at once all five forces charged forth into battle.

"Halt!" Dumbledalf cried, and all five forces promptly stopped.

"What is it now?" asked the Batman.

"We have company."

It was not a lie! It was true! Out from around the Ravens'

locker room marched five more armies, each of them boasting another king.

Billy looked upon them, exhausted by the growing number of enemies he'd need to keep an eye on. He wasn't equipped to count more than five of anything except food, which he counted in units of A Lot of Food. "But who could they be?" asked the wobbit. "I thought everyone was already here."

"Name yourselves," yelled Dumbledalf in the entirely wrong direction. "I, for one, am a wizard! A uniwizard!"

He giggled, then cried, then turned his hat backward and insisted on being called Lil-D.

The five kings approached, pushing and shoving their way to the front. Due to a lack of desirable cable options in Wobbottabad, Billy did not have HBO, and therefore did not recognize the five advancing kings. Of course, as you have likely guessed by now, they were the five final contestants in the highly competitive *Game of Musical Chairs*.

"I am Lord Joyfree Bloodbathian," said the douchiest, "Lord of the Seven Kingdoms."

"I am Lord Standin Bloodbathian," said the grumpiest, "Lord of the Seven Kingdoms."

"I am Lord Manly Bloodbathian," said the most effeminate, "Lord of the Seven Kingdoms."

"I am Lord Heartthrob Starcrossed," said the one who seemed least likely to die, "King of the North."

"I am Bailing Theonboy," said the one who would be having no grandchildren anytime soon, "King of the North and Iron Islands."

The five kings walked to the fore, coming face-to-face with the other five kings, who were all understandably annoyed because they'd already ordered their "I Survived the Battle of Five Armies and All I Got Was This Lousy Shirt" shirts.

Billy raised his hand. When no one called on him, he did not speak.

"What brings you to our battle?" asked the Batman. "We were just about to begin, and anyway, we've reached maximum capacity."

"How dare you speak so grimly to the Lord of the Seven Kingdoms!" said the first three in unison.

The original five leaders glanced at each other, confounded.

"How many kingdoms do we have, exactly?" asked Billy at last, speaking the thought on everyone's mind.

"You, uhh . . . babes . . . darlin' babies . . . donwehave four? Got fork kingdoms . . . forkins . . . ," wagered the Elvisking.

"Okay," said Billy. "So we have the Elven Lands, Jerkwood, the Mountain with Zero Friends, and the Mountains Whose Peaks Are Concealed by Gathering Precipitation Around Their Summits."

"Impossible," argued Bard. "I am the rightful heir to Fail, land of my fathers, so that's at least five."

"And surely the North has been unaccounted for," Bain pointed out. "Do you think those ten million bats came from my house? They did not come from my house."

"And Rake-town, of course," put in Nixon, who had been inexplicably reelected in a landslide. "So perhaps it is in fact seven."

"Then it is fourteen," corrected Heatthrob Starcrossed. "Your seven and our seven."

"What do you mean?" asked Dumbledalf, coincidentally at a suitable moment.

Joyfree Bloodbathian was quickly growing bored. He hadn't killed any prostitutes in this scene. "Is this not the North?"

"Of course it is the North," said Richard Nixon.

"Ain'tno notnorth . . ." added the Elvisking.

"Then we are in the right place. The North is one of our kingdoms."

"But the North is one of *our* kingdoms," asserted Bain.

"Well, then," said Heartthrob Starcrossed. "It appears we all have a kingdom in common. I will live for a long, long time."

"So it is thirteen kingdoms in all, then," said Billy, "six to the each of us and one in common. But what are the lot of you even fighting for?"

"The Pointy Chair, of course," said Standin Bloodbathian.

The shoulders of the original five leaders were growing sore from all the shrugging. Never before had they heard of any pointy chair, not even in the songs of lore, or the Top 40 songs of catchy, topical lore.

"And just what is the Pointy Chair?" asked Richard Nixon, activating a tape recorder in his suit.

"You know," said Joyfree. "The Pointy Chair. The chair everyone wants to sit in."

"Sounds uncomfortable," admitted Billy.

The kings of the Other Seven Kingdoms eyed each other.

"But . . . no," said Standin. "The Pointy Chair is, like, the best chair. I mean, literally the best."

"Sounds like it hurts," said Billy. Generations later, the songs would sing of his fierceness and courage, but really he was just calling it like he saw it.

"You don't understand," cut in Joyfree. "It's a chair built

from the swords of all the kings who died from sitting on it. It's awesome."

"Oh," said the Batman. "That does sound kind of awesome," he muttered grimly.

"I'm in," said Bain. "Let's go to war for that."

Richard Nixon could not believe what he was hearing. "But what of the Oscars and Golden Globes piled up in the Mountain with Zero Friends?"

"You don't get to zero friends without making a few enemies," shouted Sorkinshield from the mountain's front gate. He was beginning to fear they had forgotten he might have something important to say.

"Forget about some trophies to put above your fireplace," said Manly Bloodbathian. "Imagine looking at that fireplace *from the comfort of your Pointy Chair*."

"I like him the best," whispered Dumbledalf to one of his own freckles.

It appeared then that there was nothing left to discuss. The Pointy Chair was worth dying for.

"So we're all in agreement," said Billy. "The Battle of Five Armies shall hereby be the Battle of Ten Armies."

"The Battle of Five Armies?" cried Joyfree. "This is the War of Five Kings! If you very well must, we shall make it the War of Ten Kings."

"Now just a minute," interjected Bain. "I signed up for a battle, not a war—"

"Halt!" screeched Dumbledalf.

"*Now* what?" rang a chorus of self-important, inbred male voices.

But lo and behold, their question was answered on the horizon, marching in from the south—the one direction that everybody had forgotten about. Yet another five rulers—and you'll never believe this—with another five armies.

"Name yourselves," ordered Dumbledalf. "My name is Wizard."

"I am J. R. R. Toking," said the oldest. "And I am your creator."

"I am G. R. R. Marauding," said the one most likely to die before finishing his incredibly ambitious book series. "Also your creator."

"I am J. K. Rousing," said the most effeminate. "And I am somehow wrapped up in this."

"I am C. S. Losing," said the one who had no business here. "And I created a thing similar to this which should be a part of the conversation."

"I am T. H. Lampoon," said the definitely best one. "And I just wanted to point out for the last time that you can order our magazine online, follow us on Twitter, or if you feel like it, both."*

Behind them stood armies millions and millions strong, comprised of their most loyal followers gathered up from all the lands. Their ranks stretched on for countless miles, spanning the length of Jerkwood and the Forest of Metaphorical Importance and dropping off into the Vast Unknown. They were a noble race, descendants of literates, which certainly impressed Billy, who was a descendant of those who looked quizzically at microwave timers.

With all these armies, things were getting out of hand. Some warriors even went so far as to count themselves members of multiple armies, which—come on—was kind of a

---

* http://www.harvardlampoon.com, http://twitter.com/harvardlampoon, http://www.linkedin.com/daLampoonOfficialxxx

dick move. A dragon could claim itself a member of three of the armies, and a wizard, due to the magical laws of Widdle Wearth, had to pick his least favorite four. It was all quite confusing. One minute a lion was a literal lion, and the next he was presumed to be just a metaphorical lion.

"And what is it all of *you* want?" asked Richard Nixon.

"It is simple, really," said J. R. R. Toking, drawing a long puff from his pipe. "We want our characters back."

"What for?"

"To kill them," explained G. R. R. Marauding.

"This whole 'book' or what have you is really butchering our masterfully crafted characters," clarified J. K. Rousing. "So the least we can do is kill them now and spare them the humiliation of having to finish things up in some college humor magazine's idea of a fantasy story."

"Did you know I'm a devout Catholic?" asked C. S. Losing, feeling a little left out of the fun.*

"Look," said Billy. All this talk about death reminded him of dead animals, which reminded him of eating dead animals. "We've already capped this at ten armies. I'm sorry, but you've come too late. I do not wish to be rude, but you must respect that there is no room left for you."

"Nonsense," scoffed J. R. R. Toking, and he proceeded to blow a smoke ring that wrapped itself around all existence. "I built these lands myself, using an incredibly unnecessary

---

* Getting left out of the fun is, debatably, the whole point of Catholicism.†

† Finally this cross makes sense. I still don't have a clue what the other one is, though.‡

‡ You could fit a lot of Jesuses on this thing. I've never even seen the next one before. Only one way to find out . . .*

*Whoa.

amount of words. If I say so, there is certainly room for us to fight on them."

"So what shall we call this?" huffed the wobbit impatiently. "The Army Battle of the Fifteen Warring Kings?"

"Not so fast," said J. K. Rousing. She raised a hand to the back of her head and whipped off her ponytail bun.

"She's a woman!" every single person on the battlefield gasped in disbelief.

"This might go against my Catholic faith," C. S. Losing let it be known, as if anyone cared what he had to say.

"Then it is settled once and for all!" Billy beckoned. "This shall henceforth be known as the Army Battle of the Fourteen Warring Kings and One Warring Queen, and we shall fight for copyright laws, Academy Awards, and pointy chairs. Can we all now be in agreement? Please?"

"Halt!" bellowed Dumbledalf. Many tossed down their murder weapons to the ground in anger. They followed his gaze toward the west. It had been so long since they'd thought about the west that they'd forgotten all about it, though a shrewd preteen reader would have remembered that west was the direction the wind was blowing, and everyone knew what that meant.

Twenty more armies crested the western hill, asking about this awesome chair they'd heard about. They brought word that they had sent invitations to all their friends and another sixteen armies were probably on their way and all the present armies should just sit tight. They argued some more about where everyone should begin on the battlefield, as it was becoming increasingly unclear where to have the artists draw the dotted lines. Sorkinshield insisted there be time for war speeches, and the Elvisking riled up even more emotions with a few chords from his baby grand piano. Once everybody showed up, they decided to cap the thing at fifty armies, because at least the round number would look nice on the participation trophies they'd all be getting afterward.

"Hal—"

"Shut up, Hitler!" cried everyone in unison, and Hitler went trudging home sadly, dragging his army of very nice paintings behind him. Now, once and for all, the fight could finally begin.

"Thank goodness," said Billy. He slipped on his anklet and raised his fists, ready to start his first war battle.

To ensure there would be no pause to the festivities this time around, the Elvisking produced a bugle to signal the start of the slaughter. He played a dainty tune that put all into the proper mood, and turned to retreat to the safety of the traveling elven orchestra pit.

But, of course, he did not see Billy standing beside him, nervously wobbling in nauseatingly enhanced motion. The tip of the bugle's horn struck Billy straight upon the forehead, and in due course did Billy strike the ground.

That was the last of the first war battle that Billy ever saw.

XIII

The Last Stage Before the First Stage of the Books That Actually Matter,

or

There and Bored Again

When Billy finally came to, the battlefield looked much different. Gone were the gathering armies and vaguely operatic underscoring. Tired-looking men in black headphones and worn-out sweatshirts were taking down the lights as dead bodies helped each other up and headed for the craft services table. One such gruesomely slaughtered young Moblin was struggling mightily to lift up our wobbit's leg and sweating so much in the process that the gash on his forehead was beginning to melt off.

"Victory after all, I suppose!" Billy said, trying to piece together what was going on. "Well, it seems a very gloomy business."

"Whoa!" said the Moblin, jumping back in surprise. "Sorry, man, I totally thought you were a prop."

"It's me, Billy Bagboy, companion of Aaron Sorkinshield!"

"I was just looking for my phone."

"I have had a nasty knock on the head, I think. But I have a helm and a hard skull. All the same I feel sick, and my legs are like straw."

"Right . . . okay. Do you think you could call it? It's on vibrate, which I know is a total pain in the ass right now, but honestly, who wants to hear a ringtone anymore? I mean, it's 2013."*

Billy was getting more and more confused by the moment, and he decided he did not much like this dead Moblin. He swallowed the phone he had been chewing on and went to find a more familiar face. As he walked he saw many strange things. A Little Person was making out with an elf in the bushes, and two trolls were trying to sneak away as many swords and pieces of armor as possible so that they could sell them online to other sad little trolls at home. The Philadelphia Eagles were all gathered around Brian Westbrook's laptop watching *Orange Is the New Black*, and an energetic, unshaven New Zealander was hunched over a copy of *The Silmarillion* trying to figure out how many movies he could split it up into.

Finally, Billy began to find himself in more normal territory. Lights snapped on and camera angles shifted so that the Little People once again appeared little and women and minorities once again did not appear in positions of power or meaningful agency. Finally he came upon Dumbledalf outside a tent in Fail, and everything clicked back into the right kind of complete nonsense.

---

* 2014 if you were given this book as a Christmas present and let it fester for six days before peeling open the cover.

"Dementia! Dementia!" cried Dumbledalf, smacking Billy across the face with a dead pigeon.

"It's just me!" said Billy.

That clarified things for Dumbledalf, and a smile broke out across the old man's face as he recognized Billy and ran to embrace him. He was a very great wizard and an even better hugger, and even now it is the only time in all of Widdle Wearth lore that anyone has successfully wrapped their arms completely around a wobbit. Legend has it that Billy's heart grew three sizes that day, which was a full size larger than the two sizes Billy's heart grew every other day.

"The Boy Who Is Alive," exclaimed Dumbledalf. "That's so much better than what I was calling you before: The Boy Who Was Here a Few Minutes Ago, What's His Name, The One with the Thing on His Face."

Billy told Dumbledalf that he was glad to see him too, and inquired as to the rest of their party. At this, Dumbledalf grew suddenly serious. He put his pants back on and led Billy into the tent. There lay Aaron Sorkinshield, paler than Billy had ever seen him. During the battle he had eaten some strange mushrooms, and, mistaking a battalion of especially old, white trolls for angry Republicans, had thrown himself off the Mountain with Zero Friends. He had hit rock bottom, bounced a few times, and landed next to a pool of self-reflection. Now all his various bags of writing powders and inspiration rocks lay open and empty on the floor around him. He trembled in his bed with his eyes closed. When Billy entered, he opened them and smiled faintly.

"Farewell, good wobbit," he said. "I go now to the halls of sobriety, to sit beside my brothers in suffering in a little circle until the world is renewed, or at least until twenty-six days have passed. I wish to part in friendship from you, and also I will soon be required to make amends. So let me say this: there is more in you of good than you know, and I don't just mean all the Mr. Goodbars I know you stole from my pack. If more of us valued food above hoarded gold and fancy clothing and social standing and the ability to stand or walk or live past middle age, it would be a merrier world."*

"Thank you, Aaron Sorkinshield," said Billy, tears welling up in his eyes. The silence was a little awkward since the orchestra had gone home. Sorkinshield took his hand and the two travelers smiled at each other. Then Sorkinshield cleared his throat.

"And . . ." he prompted.

"And?"

The Little Person gestured to himself meaningfully. Billy laughed, glad to see that his friend had not changed too much.

"And I am sorry to see you go," he said. "With or without your powder and your rocks and your occasionally redundant tropes, you are a truly great writer. As far as Little People go, you may be the biggest."

With these words, a little of Sorkinshield's self-important color returned to his cheeks, and he closed his eyes again and lay back down on the bed, already dreaming of the awards and accolades this scene would receive. Billy patted him on the head, took away the potion Dumbledalf was making out of Sorkinshield's remaining mushrooms, and left the tent.

---

* Would it? Book circles and prison reading groups, discuss. This might be an especially instructive question for those on death row—that last meal is coming up, boys!

All that had happened after he was stunned, Billy learned later, but it brought him more confusion than clarity, as Dumbledalf kept mixing it up with another battle in which he had lost his weasel in a dusty hollow. Still, he managed to piece together a rough sketch of what went on:

Even with the Eagles and the Ravens running a nearly flawless passing game, the Little People and the Elves and the Humans found themselves outnumbered by the Moblins and the wargis and those forty-five other armies that had eventually joined in. That was when Björn appeared—no one knew how or from where, but it was hardly the first deus ex machina they had dealt with and certainly wouldn't be the last. Whatever machine gave birth to this golden god, though, they were thankful for it, for Björn was in full Swede mode. His music was even catchier than Billy remembered, and he danced and fought with yet wilder abandon.

Björn found Sorkinshield crumpled up and tripping out at the pool of self-reflection, and his pain struck a chord with the Swede just as the Elvisking was striking a powerful blues chord in the field below. *He had learned the worst lesson that life can teach—that it makes no sense. And when that happens, happiness is never spontaneous again. It is artificial and, even then, bought at the price of an obstinate estrangement from oneself and one's history.** He carried his fallen friend to the tent by the Old Rimrock and rejoined the fight with even greater fury and disillusionment.

Meanwhile, the Army Battle of the Forty-Nine Warring Kings and One Warring Queen had grown as confounding as one might expect. The five newly arrived kings seemed far

---

* This moral brought to you by Philip Roth and Pepsi-Cola. Pepsi: Come Alive! You're in the Pepsi Generation.

more interested in gratuitous nudity and elaborate exposition than actually resolving anything, and it didn't help their chances in battle when they froze after every hour and called it a cliffhanger. The Moblins became rather fascinated with this, and more and more of them gave up fighting to see how the *Game of Musical Chairs* would play out. Then, after a particularly bloody cliffhanger, the kings stopped and looked at one another, embarrassed. None of them had actually read the books, so no one knew what was going to happen next. The Moblins solved this problem by killing them all and taking G. R. R. Marauding prisoner, forcing him to write in more death scenes until they were satisfied.

From there, things only descended into further chaos. Kiwi was killed by deforestation and invasive mammalian predators, and Fili was killed by an arrow through his face. C. S. Losing put his faith in God, Richard Nixon put Puff's treasure into a slush fund, and Hitler passive-aggressively threw paper airplanes at anyone who passed by his secret Hitler hole. J. K. Rousing became fed up with the lack of gender parity and exited, leaving only a casual vacancy where once you could have heard her cuckoo calling. At one point, the whole affair seemed like it was running out of steam, with Bain and Bard the Batman exchanging only halfhearted punches in the stomach and L. Ron and Elvisking exchanging secrets on how to make massive amounts of white people go insane. Then Kendrick Valar, a godlike creature with the flow of a thousand rivers and the beats of a thousand thunders, descended from the heavens. He delivered a single, perfect verse, then ascended once again, having single-handedly reignited the battle below him and made all YOLOs seem rather silly.

The Moblins and their allies fought valiantly, but in the end they were no match for the fact that the good guys always win. The treasure of Oscars and Emmys and Golden Globes was split up evenly between Billy and Dumbledalf and all the remaining Little People—except Drawlin and Ballin, who were left with one People's Choice Award to share. Drawlin argued that this was because they had not been forceful enough in claiming the treasure, while Ballin countered that they were facing a history of treasurelessness combined with insidious flaws in the treasure-distribution system. Meanwhile, Whorey, Slorey, and Kourtney posed with their new bling, Beefer and Buffer melted theirs into solid gold barbells, Loin and Groin gave very sincere acceptance speeches, and Doc died of consumption.

This left only Dumbledalf and Billy, who was now very eager to get home. The Gram side of him had begun to get worn out, and the Bagboy side of him reminded him that he had probably missed at least one shift at the store. The pair briefly considered going back the way they'd come, through dozens of dangers and thousands of miles, and months and months of character development. But their newly acquired treasure was heavy and they were both a little drunk.* They decided to take the high-speed rail instead.†

As they boarded the convenient and reasonably priced bullet train from Fail to Wobbottabad, Billy waved good-bye to all the strange and wonderful people he had met. Richard Nixon

---

* Dumbledalf had recently introduced Billy to his favorite cocktail: a pint of beer with a stick of butter thrown in. Unsurprisingly, Billy was an immediate fan.

† The high-speed rail was an environmentally friendly, economically viable investment made by the Humans at the dawning of the Third Age. It was courageously approved via ballot proposition and bond measure, despite the opposition of Sauron Musk, Dark CEO of the Hyper Doom.

flashed him a V for "victory" and Whorey flashed him her V for "professional reasons." He was sad to leave every one of them, except Ballin and Drawlin, who still made him feel the uncomfortable obligation to examine his personal shortcomings and societal responsibilities. As he raced back home at an average speed of 180 mph (290 km/h), he saw all the hills and valleys he had passed through on his journey. He saw the river where he and the Little People had—well, never mind, he passed that too quickly. But up here was where he heroically—nope, missed it. Darn it, that was a really cool—oh! Oh! Right here! That was the thing with the spi—nope, gone. At least as they drew near to Livinwell, he knew he would be able to hear one last song of convenient plot summary from the beautiful Celebritologists living there:

The dra—

And then at last Billy was home, convinced by the train's efficiency, if not its narrative function. He and Dumbledalf, who had spent the better part of the ride sketching pictures of Billy posing naked with horses, now stepped off the platform and into Wobbottabad, where the shapes of the land and trees were as well-known to him as the arrhythmic beats of his heart. Coming to the beginning of the town-wide downhill slope (one of the proudest and only accomplishments in the history of wobbit urban planning), he stopped suddenly and said:

Franchises go ever ever on,
Over-budget and under-seen,
Through sequels that are quickly gone,
And prequels that never should have been;
And filmmakers who work on an epic scale

(As to old habits they resort)
Forget they're adapting a children's tale,
That was all the better for being short.

Yes, franchises go ever ever on,
Over-budget and under-seen,
As cameras sweep from dusk to dawn,
And fanboys drool over every scene;
Yet before you adapt every chapter and letter,
One word of advice you'd be wise to keep:
A child may very well imagine something better,
Once your saga sends him off to sleep.

Dumbledalf looked over at him. "My dear Hairy!" he said. "Something is the matter with you! You are not the wobbit that you once were."

Billy smiled slightly, but was already regretting speaking the rhymes instead of singing them. He turned to face his wizard friend.

"Never mind," retracted Dumbledalf. "I was just looking at you from behind."

And so they made their way through town, past the Mc-Donald's and the McDonald's Express, past the McCafé and the old folks home, which had been converted into a Super McDonald's after all the old folks started dying young from eating too much McDonald's. Then they came right to Billy's door—or at least where the door should have been.

"That's odd," said Billy. "I don't remember eating that." He rolled into his home, only to find that there was not much home left to roll into. There was only an empty hole, robbed of all Billy's refrigerators and mini refrigerators and meat lockers and mini-meat lockers. Everything was gone, down to the smallest crumb, and Billy knew exactly where he kept all his crumbs. The only thing of note left in the whole hole was a note:

You take my livelihood, I take your life. That's the burgling way, buddy, and I don't care if you like it!

Your well-qualified burglar neighbor,
Craig

P.S. For tax reasons, I've attached a list of everything I took. I'm a burglar, not an inconveniencer!

As Billy read through Craig's list, which also contained some strange offers for "adult services," he reflected on just how little he'd lost compared to how much he had gained. Specifically, he had lost a lot of mostly expired foodstuffs and gained an incredible amount of priceless treasure. This cheered Billy immensely, for he had not yet learned that universal truth which the Notorious J. R. R. put so well.*

It turned out, though, that Billy had lost a lot more than just material goods. He had lost his reputation. It was as though no one remembered how respectable he used to be, because that was exactly the case: three generations of wobbits had come and passed while Billy was getting regular exercise.

Still, Billy found that he didn't much care. People's opinions of you only matter as much as the people who have them, and wobbits were best known for taking up a lot of matter and mattering very little. So Billy used a part of his treasure to buy

---

* Mo' Money, Mo' Ringwraiths.

some of the fancy organic food he had tasted at Livinwell, and the rest of it he spent on a treadmill, so that he could spend every day walking and talking and pretending he was back on another quest without ever leaving the safety of his uncluttered hole. And though few other wobbits believed any of his tales, all of which seemed cardiovascularly inconceivable, he remained very happy to the end of his days, and those were extraordinarily long.

One autumn evening some years afterward, Billy was sitting in his study, formerly his swallowing cubicle, and writing his memoirs, which he was thinking of calling *There and Bored Again: A Book You Should Buy for Everyone You Know*. Just then there was a knock at his newly installed, unsalted rice-cake door. It was Dumbledalf, and, in preparation for an epilogue, he had brought unconvincing old-man makeup and two children he insisted belonged to Billy, though they were actually just Loin and Groin.

"Come in! Come in!" said Billy, who rarely got visitors now that he had put in a flight of stairs where the rolling path used to be. They sat down around the only dining room table and fell to talking of their times together. Billy asked how things were going in the lands of the Mountain with Zero Friends, which they told him had gotten a lot more popular ever since wobal warming had melted all the silly-looking snow off its head. Bard the Batman had rebuilt the town of Fail as a gritty, critically acclaimed metropolis, and Richard Nixon had finally been run out of Rake-town after he was discovered secretly spying on the beloved Rake. Ballin had been elected the new master of Rake-town, and, though adored by the majority, he was bitterly opposed by a group of Ents calling themselves the Tree Party. He even faced a good deal of criticism from

Drawlin, who viewed his election as a sign of progress, but also a potential excuse for certain Tree Partiers' claim they were living in a postracial society.

"And Hermione has gotten really, really hot," added Dumbledalf. "What about you, Hairy? How have you passed your indiscriminate amount of time?"

Billy described all the ways in which his life had changed. He could now change his shirt without any assistance, and even buy new shirts without having to shop in the bedsheets section. He was able to hop short distances into the air and catch a ball without having to catch his breath. But talking to Dumbledalf made Billy realize how much he had missed companionship, however senile. Maybe what had made him so happy in the wake of his YOLO was not the loss of so much weight, but the gaining of so many friends. After all, when you step on the scales of life, that's the only number that really matters. People with no friends go to hell.

"I just don't feel like I fit in here anymore," Billy sighed. "I even lost my job at the grocery store—I can no longer call myself a Bagboy!"

At this, the last remaining twinkle in Dumbledalf's eye did its little dance.

"My dear Hairy," he said. "If you don't fit in here, we'll just take you somewhere else! Never underestimate people's capacity to adjust. Take me, for example: I died halfway through this book and they just replaced me with another old white guy!"*

---

* Now's a good time to announce that the role of Dumbledalf, normally played by American sweetheart Regis Philbin, will instead be played by Sir Michael Gambon riding on the shoulders of Sir Ian McKellan for chapters ✿ through thirteen. The *Harvard Lampoon* thanks you for your understanding.

So Dumbledalf led Billy across The Street and over The Bump and into another town that Billy had somehow never noticed before. It looked almost exactly like Wobbottabad, but all of its references were outdated and all of its jokes were better respected. It was almost as though it had been inexplicably reissued from the late 1960s, in the hopes that people might buy it again, or buy it for the first time and be really confused.

"Welcome to Bag Eye," announced Dumbledalf. "Home of the boggies!"

Billy looked around, enchanted by the strange sights and sounds all about him. And there was Puff! The fierce dragon reared its head in a lonely corner to the tune of a controversial electric guitar, sniffing one more chance at friendship.

Alas, there was still one thing bothering our good wobbit.

"What shall I call myself?" he asked. "I'm not a Bagboy anymore, and all my heroism has left me feeling far from a Billy."

There it was. The moment. Loin and Groin reached deep within themselves, into the most hallowed recesses of their sophomoric minds. They took a deep, sensual breath. Then time stood still and fate finally relieved itself all over everybody:

"Dildo Bugger," they said in unison, and then they died, with stupid, idiotic smiles plastered across their stupid, idiotic faces.

And so the newly christened Dildo prepared to start his new life in the town of Bag Eye. He turned to the wizard who had given him so much while making so little sense.

"Thank you, Dumbledalf." He smiled. "I don't know how I'll ever repay—ow!"

"Sorry," said Dumbledalf sheepishly, removing the sword from Dildo's leg. "I was so sure you were a Horcrux."

ABOUT *THE HARVARD LAMPOON*

Founded in 1876, the *Harvard Lampoon* is a semi-secret Sorrento Square social organization that used to occasionally publish a so-called humor magazine.[*] At the time of its debut, United States President Ulysses S. Grant was advised not to read the publication, as he would be too much "in stitches" to run the government. Now the world's oldest continuously published comedy magazine, its alumni have gone on to write for *Saturday Night Live*, *The Simpsons*, *The Office*, *30 Rock*, and *The Tonight Show with Jay Leno*. The *Harvard Lampoon* is also the proud author of the classic parodies *The Hunger Pains*, *Bored of the Rings*, and *Nightlight*, as well as curator of the infamous Joke-A-Boom Zone, wherein all fines double.

---

[*] Samuels, Robert R., "Newspapers Going Out of Business." *The Harvard Crimson,* November 31, 2013.

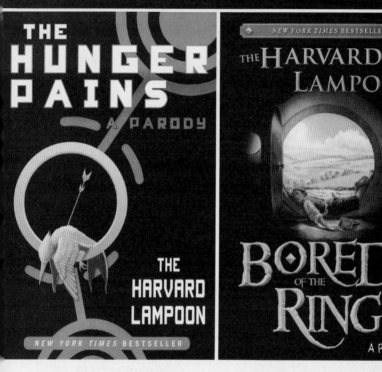